Mind Renewal in a Mindless Age

Also by James Montgomery Boice

Witness and Revelation in the Gospel of John
Philippians: An Expositional Commentary
The Sermon on the Mount
How to Live the Christian Life
  (originally, *How to Live It Up*)
Ordinary Men Called by God
  (originally, *How God Can Use Nobodies*)
The Last and Future World
The Gospel of John: An Expositional Commentary
  (5 volumes in one)
"Galatians" in the *Expositor's Bible Commentary*
Can You Run Away from God?
Our Sovereign God, editor
Our Savior God: Studies on Man, Christ
  and the Atonement, editor
Does Inerrancy Matter?
The Foundation of Biblical Authority, editor
Making God's Word Plain, editor
The Epistles of John
Genesis: An Expositional Commentary (3 volumes)
The Parables of Jesus
The Christ of Christmas
The Minor Prophets: An Expositional Commentary
  (2 volumes)
Standing on the Rock
The Christ of the Empty Tomb
Foundations of the Christian Faith (4 volumes in one)
Christ's Call to Discipleship
Transforming Our World: A Call to Action, editor
Ephesians: An Expositional Commentary
Daniel: An Expositional Commentary
Joshua: We Will Serve the Lord
Nehemiah: Learning to Lead
The King Has Come
Romans (3 volumes)
Amazing Grace

Mind Renewal in a Mindless Age

Preparing to Think and Act Biblically

A Study of Romans 12:1–2

James Montgomery Boice

Baker Books

A Division of Baker Book House Co.
Grand Rapids, Michigan 49516

Copyright © 1993 by James Montgomery Boice

Published by Baker Books
a division of Baker Book House Company
P.O. Box 6287, Grand Rapids, MI 49516-6287

Third printing, February 1995

Printed in the United States of America

Library of Congress Cataloging-in-Publication Data

Boice, James Montgomery, 1938–
    Mind renewal in a mindless age: preparing to think and act
biblically / James Montgomery Boice.
        p.   cm.
    Includes bibliographical references.
    ISBN 0-8010-1068-3
    1. Bible. N.T. Romans—Criticism, interpretation, etc. 2. Church
and the world—Biblical teaching. I. Title.
    BS2665.2.B65 1993
    227'.106—dc20   93-13459

To **HIM**
whose "mind" also needs
to be found in us

Contents

Preface

We live in mindless times, days in which millions of people are drifting along through life, manipulated by the mass media, particularly television, and hardly know it. Few give thought for their eternal souls, and most, even Christians, are unaware of any way of thinking or living other than that of the secular culture that surrounds them. Fortunately, scattered here and there are people who yearn after God and want their lives to be different from the lives of mere humanists, materialists, and secularists. They want their lives to count for God.

Are you one of these people? I think you must be. Or at least, you may be on your way to becoming one. Otherwise you would probably not have picked up this book. I want to commend a careful reading of it to you.

Americans are a practical people. That is good! But we are not a particularly strong-thinking people, and that is bad, since what we do practically always flows from our minds and therefore needs to be directed by our thinking.

The apostle Paul was practical. The last halves of most of his letters contain practical directions for how Christians are to live the Christian life. But it is significant that the first halves all contain strong doctrine, obviously because Paul was aware that what we think will determine what we do. In fact, in the great Book of Romans, at the very start of the section that the editors of *The NIV Study Bible* list in their outline as "Righteousness Practiced," Paul begins with a challenge to us to be transformed by the renewing of our minds.

> Therefore, I urge you, brothers, in view of God's mercy, to offer your bodies as living sacrifices, holy and pleasing to God—this is your spiritual act of worship. Do not conform any longer to the pattern of this world, but be transformed by the renewing of your mind. Then you will be able to test and approve what God's will is—his good, pleasing and perfect will.
>
> Romans 12:1–2

This book is about those two verses, and it is an urgent call for you and every other serious Christian to get on with that task.

It is a process, of course. It is not something we can accomplish in a few years of study, still less in a few short hours of reading. But it is important that we begin, and even first steps are valuable. I assure you that, if you do begin, you will find the journey you are on to be the most fascinating and rewarding of any that you have ever taken in your life, for you will be learning to think like God—and become like God, too.

James Montgomery Boice

How Should We Then Live?

"Therefore, I urge you, brothers"

> *As Christians we are not only to know the right*
> *world view . . . but consciously to act upon that*
> *world view so as to influence society in all its*
> *parts and facets across the whole spectrum of*
> *life, as much as we can to the extent of our indi-*
> *vidual and collective ability.*
>
> Francis A. Schaeffer

Harry Blamires is an Englishman who has written an important Christian book titled *The Christian
Mind: How Should a Christian Think?*[1] He was a student
of C. S. Lewis, and his book was first published in 1963,
thirty years ago. Its main thesis, repeated over and over
in chapter 1, is that "there is no longer a Christian mind."
Blamires meant by this that in our time there is no longer

a distinctly Christian way of thinking. There is to some extent a Christian ethic and even a somewhat Christian way of life and piety. But there is no distinctly Christian frame of reference, no uniquely Christian world view to guide our thinking in distinction from the thoughts of the secular world around us.

Unfortunately, the situation has not improved over the past thirty years. In fact, it has grown worse. Today, not only is there little or no genuine Christian thinking, there is very little thinking of any kind, and the western world (and perhaps even the world as a whole) is well on its way to becoming what I and many others have frequently called a "mindless society."

What a challenge to today's Christians! It is a challenge because we are called to think, even though the world around us does not think or at best thinks in non-Christian categories. The best statement of that challenge is the powerful statement that the apostle Paul provides in the great opening paragraph of Romans 12. He calls it mind renewal:

> Therefore, I urge you, brothers, in view of God's mercy, to offer your bodies as living sacrifices, holy and pleasing to God—this is your spiritual act of worship. Do not conform any longer to the pattern of this world, but be transformed by the renewing of your mind. Then you will be able to test and approve what God's will is—his good, pleasing and perfect will.

These two verses introduce what has often been called the "practical" section of Paul's letter. But I do not like that way of talking about it. What people usually mean by using that word here is that the first eleven chapters of Romans are doctrinal or theological, and that the letter finally gets down to practical matters at this point. But doctrine is practical, and practical material must be doctrinal if it is to be of any help at all. A far better way to talk about Romans 12 through 16 is to say that these chapters contain *applications* of the very practical teachings or doctrines that Paul presented earlier.

"Application" is the word that John Murray, one of the best modern interpreters of Romans, uses in his introduction to this section: "At this point the apostle comes to deal with concrete practical application."[2]

Or maybe an even better word is "consequences," which occurs to me because of the compelling slogan of the Hillsdale College newsletter *Imprimis*: "Because Ideas Have Consequences." We have had many ideas in the first great sections of Romans—truthful ideas, stirring ideas, ideas that have come to us by means of an inerrant and authoritative revelation—and now we are to explore their consequences.

Whose Values? And Why?

The first and most important consequence is that, if a person really understands and believes what Paul has written, he or she will begin to think differently about everything.

Let me make this point still another way by saying that "consequences" is also the significance of the word *then* in the title of Francis Schaeffer's well-known study of the rise and fall of western culture, *How Should We Then Live?* Schaeffer, recognized internationally for his studies and writings in philosophy, was best known for his ability to communicate biblical truths to diverse groups of people. Nowhere is his gift for finding relevance in the words of the Bible seen more clearly than in this book's title, which is taken from God's instructions to the priest-prophet Ezekiel regarding the Israelites, who had fallen into idolatry and moral corruption:

> Therefore, O thou son of man [Ezekiel], speak unto the
> house of Israel; Thus ye speak, saying, If our transgres-
> sions and our sins be upon us, and we pine away in them,
> *how should we then live?* Say unto them, As I live, saith
> the Lord God, I have no pleasure in the death of the
> wicked; but that the wicked turn from his way and live;
> turn ye, turn ye from your evil ways. . . .
>
> Ezekiel 33:10–11 KJV

"Then" is such a very simple word that we hardly think
twice about how we use it. But when we reflect on the
title and contents of *How Should We Then Live?* it is
clear at once that "then" is the pivotal and most important word. Suppose the book were called simply "How
Should We Live?" There would be nothing remarkable
about that. It's a common enough question, not much
different from asking, "What shall we do today?" Or
"Where shall we have dinner tonight?" But put the
"then" into the title and the question becomes: "How
shall we live in light of the fact that God has redeemed
us from sin's penalty by the death of Jesus Christ and
freed us from sin's tyranny by the power of the Holy
Spirit?"

About twenty years ago, when *How Should We Then
Live?* was published, Schaeffer was very clear about
where he thought western culture was headed. He looked
at such trends as increasing economic breakdown, violence in all areas of life and all countries, extreme
poverty for many of the Third World's peoples, a love of
affluence, and the underlying relativism of western
thought. And he concluded that the choice before
humanity was either totalitarianism—that is, an imposed
but arbitrary social order—or "once again affirming that
base which gave freedom without chaos in the first
place—God's revelation in the Bible and his revelation
through Christ."[3]

Here is Schaeffer's point: *Those who have received this revelation must also act on it, because that is the very nature of the revelation. It demands application.* Writes Schaeffer, "As Christians we are not only to *know* the right world view, the world view that tells us the truth of what *is,* but consciously to *act* upon that world view so as to influence society in all its parts and facets across the whole spectrum of life, as much as we can to the extent of our individual and collective ability."[4]

We are hearing a great deal about "family values" today, particularly from politicians. It was a major theme of the 1992 presidential campaign, and the Republicans used it to cast doubt on Bill Clinton's morality. I believe in family values. I supported Vice-President Dan Quayle in what he said about them during the campaign. I think he and most of our past and present leaders want the right thing for our country. But I have to say here that an appeal to "family values" without a corresponding acknowledgment of God's existence, God's law, and the biblical revelation as a basis for our standards, however well meaning, will always have a hollow ring and sound purely political and manipulative, which is what an election-time call for family values really is, in spite of the best of intentions.

I repeat, I believe in "family values." But unless we acknowledge God and his saving acts as the source and basis for these values, anyone who thinks clearly may refute our concern with such questions as: "What kind of 'family values' are we talking about? A nuclear family? A single-parent family? A homosexual family? Why should any one 'family' be preferred above another? Or why should we want a family-oriented society at all?" In other words, any call for values always invites some rejoinders: "*Whose* values are we talking about?" and "*Why* those?"

During a meeting of college educators at Harvard University in 1987, President Frank Rhodes of Cornell University suggested in an address on educational reforms that it was time for the universities to pay attention to "values" and the students' "moral well-being." At once there were gasps from the audience, and one student jumped to his feet demanding indignantly, "Whose values are to be taught? And who is to teach us?" The audience applauded loudly, which meant that in its judgment the student had rendered the president's suggestion foolish by those seemingly unanswerable questions.

President Rhodes sat down without even trying to answer them.[5]

A generation or so ago, it would have been natural for an educator to at least point to the accumulated wisdom of more than two millennia of western history—to the writings of philosophers like Plato, Socrates, and Aristotle, to historians and modern thinkers, even if not to the Bible, though many would have included it as well. It is for a return to precisely this type of education that Allan Bloom called so eloquently in his book *The Closing of the American Mind*.[6]

But all this has been forfeited today, as President Rhodes' capitulation showed. And it is not just that "times have changed" or that people today are skeptical about ever finding answers to certain questions. The problem is that without the absolutes provided by God's revelation of himself and his ways, all values are relative. With a godless world view, there is no real reason for doing one thing rather than another—except for selfish, personal reasons, an attitude that obviously destroys morality rather than establishes it. In other words, our days have become like the times of the Jewish judges when there was no king, the law was forgotten and, as a result, "everyone did as he [or she] saw fit" (Judg. 21:25).

If revelation is the basis for social morality and ethics, it is impossible to have valid, effective, or lasting values without it. We must have the doctrines set forth in Romans 1–11 in order to understand and act upon Romans 12–16.

John Calvin knew this and spoke about it at the start of his lectures on Romans 12 when he was comparing Christianity and philosophy. He said, "This is the main difference between the Gospel and philosophy. Although the philosophers speak on the subject of morals splendidly and with praiseworthy ability, yet all the embellishment which shines forth in their precepts is nothing more than a beautiful superstructure without a foundation, for by omitting principles, they propound a mutilated doctrine, like a body without a head. . . . Paul [in Romans 12:1–2] lays down the principle from which all the parts of holiness flow."[7]

"Therefore"

I have already commented on Francis Schaeffer's book *How Should We Then Live?*, saying that "then" is the all-important word. Now I note that when we come to the first verse of Romans 12, we discover exactly the same idea of consequences, only in this case the important word is "therefore." Paul writes, "*Therefore,* I urge you, brothers, in view of God's mercy, to offer your bodies as living sacrifices." He means, "In view of what I have just been writing, you must not live for yourselves but rather give yourselves wholly to God."

I am sure you have heard some teacher say at one time or another that when you come to the word *therefore* in the Bible you should always pay close attention to it, because it is "there for" a purpose. That may be a silly way of making the point, but it is a valid point. Because "therefore" always points back to something else, this means that we can never understand the importance of what is coming, or the connection between what is coming and what has been said, until we know exactly what the "therefore" is referring to.

What does the "therefore" of Romans 12:1 mean? Does it refer to the immediately preceding verses, to the doxology that ends Romans 11? Is it the whole of the eleventh chapter, in which Paul explains the wisdom of God's saving acts in history and argues for the eventual restoration of Israel? Is it Romans 8, with its stirring assertion that nothing in heaven or earth will be able to separate us from the love of God in Christ Jesus? Or, to go back even further, is it the doctrine of justification by faith expounded in chapters 1 through 4?

There have been able defenders of each of these views, as you can easily imagine. And with reason! Each can be defended by good arguments and can even be aptly illustrated.

One summer, after I had been teaching the Book of Romans to a group of teaching leaders from Bible Study Fellowship, I received a letter in which a woman thanked me for the series and explained how she had finally come to understand the importance of God's grace in election. She wrote that for years she had considered election strange and dangerous, but that now her eyes had been opened. She wrote, "Not only was my mind opened, my heart was touched. The tears were impossible to restrict several times as I realized what a privileged and totally undeserving recipient of God's grace I am. I can hardly believe what a gift I have received from him. It truly brings me to say, 'Yes, yes, yes' to Romans 12:1–2. It's the very least and only rational thing we can do in light of God's unimaginable gift."

This woman was moved by the doctrine of election, which is taught in Romans 9–11. But actually, the answer to what the "therefore" of Romans 12:1 refers is probably not election alone but *everything* in the Book of Romans that precedes it.

Charles Hodge summarizes by writing wisely and correctly, "All the doctrines of justification, grace, election, and final salvation, taught in the preceding part of the epistle, are made the foundation for the practical duties enjoined in this."[8]

This is Paul's normal pattern in his letters. In Ephesians, the first three doctrinal chapters are followed by three chapters dealing with spiritual gifts, morality, personal relationships, and spiritual warfare. In Galatians, the doctrinal section in chapters 3 and 4 is followed in chapters 5 and 6 by material on Christian liberty, spiritual fruit, love, and the obligation to do good. In Colossians, the doctrinal material is in 1:1–2:5. The application is in 2:5–4:18. The same pattern occurs in 1 and 2 Thessalonians. It is also in 1 and 2 Corinthians and in Philippians, though it is not so apparent in those letters. (Strikingly, this does not seem to be the case with the other New Testament writers—Peter and John, for example. It seems to have a special emphasis with Paul.)

Leon Morris says, "It is fundamental to [Paul] that the justified man does not live in the same way as the unrepentant sinner."[9]

This is what Paul develops in Romans 12:1–2. Just as God is the basis of reality—so that everything flows from him and takes its form from him ("For from him and through him and to him are all things," Rom. 11:36)—so also our relationship to God is the basis of all other relationships, and our duty to him the basis of all other duties. Because this is so, Paul sets out the principles that should govern our relationship to God in verses 1 and 2, reminding us that we are not our own and that we should therefore present ourselves to God as willing and living sacrifices.

The New Humanity

As we plunge into these two verses we will be seeing that everything God has done for us in salvation has bearing on everything we should think and do, that is, on all of life. We must think differently, and we must also *be* different, because God has saved us from our sins.

And Christians are different. In 1981 the Gallup Poll organization devised a scale to sort out those for whom religion seemed to be important and find out if it made any difference in their lives. Although many claim that America is a very religious country, our nation is increasingly immoral. George Gallup wanted to know if people who regarded themselves as "highly spiritually motivated" or committed to religious faith had distinctive characteristics.

He found that 12.5 percent of Americans are in this "upper" category, one person in eight. And he found that they really are different, so much so that he called them "a breed apart." The findings showed that these people differed from the rest of the population in at least four key areas.

1. They are more satisfied with their lot in life. They are happier. Sixty-eight percent said they are "very happy," as compared with only 30 percent of those who are uncommitted.

2. Their families are stronger. The divorce rate among this group is far lower than among the less committed.

3. They tend to be more tolerant of persons of different races and religions. This is exactly opposite from what the media suggest when dealing with religious people and their spiritual leaders.

4. They are more involved in charitable activities than are their nonreligious counterparts. A total of 46 percent of the highly spiritually committed said they were presently working among the poor, the infirm, and

the elderly, compared to only 36 percent among the moderately committed, 28 percent among the moderately uncommitted, and 22 percent among the highly uncommitted.[10]

True conversion does make a difference in a person's life. It is spelled out in Romans. Laws in themselves change nothing, or at least very little. It is changed people who change everything, and the only thing that ever really changes people is God himself through the gospel of our Lord Jesus Christ. If you have been called to faith in Jesus Christ, you are part of a radically changed community, the new humanity. Being part of it, it is your privilege to begin to think differently from those who are not and thus begin to make some very needed changes in our world.

Dying, We Live

"to offer your bodies as *living sacrifices*"

We are redeemed by the Lord for the purpose of consecrating ourselves and all our members to him.

John Calvin

I do not like the word *paradox* used in reference to Christian teachings, because to most people that word refers to something that is self-contradictory or false. Christianity is not false. But the dictionary also defines "paradox" as a statement that seems to be contradictory, yet may be true in fact, and in that sense there are many paradoxes in Christianity. The most obvious is the doctrine of the Trinity. We speak of one God, but we also say that God exists in three persons: God the Father, God the Son, and God the Holy Spirit. We know the doctrine of the Trinity is true because God has revealed it to be true, but we are foolish if we pretend we understand it or can explain it adequately.

One of the greatest paradoxes of Christianity concerns the Christian life: specifically the teaching that we must die in order to live. Although we find this in many places in the Bible, particularly in the New Testament,[1] the foundational statement is by Jesus, who said, "If anyone would come after me, he must deny himself and take up his cross daily and follow me. For whoever wants to save his life will lose it, but whoever loses his life for me will save it" (Luke 9:23–24).

These words inspired the well-known prayer of Saint Francis of Assisi, which concludes:

> O Divine Master, grant that I may not so much
>   Seek to be consoled as to console;
>   To be understood as to understand;
>   To be loved as to love;
>   For it is in giving that we receive;
>   It is in pardoning that we are pardoned;
> And it is in dying that we are born to eternal life.

That prayer is a statement of the principles that govern the Christian life. But it is also a good expression of what Paul sets down at the start of Romans 12 as the very first principle of all: self-sacrifice. He says, "Therefore, I urge you, brothers, in view of God's mercy, to offer your bodies as living sacrifices, holy and pleasing to God—this is your spiritual act of worship." In the cultural climate of Paul's day, both Jewish and Gentile, a sacrifice was an animal that was presented to a priest to be killed. So what Paul is saying by this striking metaphor is that the Christian life begins by our offering ourselves to God for death, but that in a paradoxical fashion it is in such an offering of ourselves that we are actually enabled to live for him and for others.

Or even stronger: It is by dying that we are enabled to live, *period*. For, as Jesus said, trying to live, if it is living for ourselves, is actually death, while dying to self is actually the way to full living. What should we call this paradox? I call it "life-by-dying" or, as I have titled this study: "Dying, We Live."

Bought with a Price

"Life-by-dying" is so foundational to the doctrine of the Christian life that we must be careful to lay it out correctly, and to do that we need to review the essential points of this principle. After that, we will go on to look at (1) the specific nature of this "sacrifice," that it is a sacrifice of our bodies presented to God as something holy and pleasing to him; and (2) the specific motive for this sacrifice: why we should make it.

The first basis for this foundational teaching is that if we are truly Christians, we are not our own but, rather, belong to Jesus. Here is the way Paul puts it in 1 Corinthians: "Do you not know that your body is a temple of the Holy Spirit, who is in you, whom you have received from God? You are not your own; you were bought with a price . . ." (1 Cor. 6:19–20). Again, just a chapter later: "You were bought at a price; do not become slaves of men" (1 Cor. 7:23). Then, if we ask what that "price" is, well, the apostle Peter tells us in the clearest possible language in his first letter: "For you know that it was not with perishable things such as silver or gold that you were redeemed from the empty way of life handed down to you from your forefathers, but with the precious blood of Christ, a lamb without blemish or defect" (1 Peter 1:18–19).

In that passage Peter used the important word *redemption,* which is the act of "buying back" or "being bought again." This is one of the key words for describing what the Lord Jesus Christ accomplished for us by his death on the cross.

What exactly did Jesus do on the cross? The biblical answer is that he paid the price of our redemption. Since this word refers to buying something or someone, the image is of a slave market in which we who are sinners are being offered to whoever will pay the highest price for us. The world is ready to bid, particularly if we are attractive or in some other way valuable by its standards. But the world bids in its own currency, which is a very debased coinage.

It bids *fame.* Worldly people sell their souls for fame; some people will do anything to be well known.

It bids *wealth.* Millions believe that making money is the most important thing any person can do, for they think that money will buy anything.

It bids *power.* Many people are crazy for power today; they are on a power-trip.

It bids *sex.* Many have lost nearly everything of value in life for just one moment of indulgence.

But into the midst of this vast "vanity fair" of a marketplace, Jesus comes, and the price he bids to rescue enslaved sinners is his blood. He offers to die for them. God, who controls this "auction," as he controls everything else, says, "Sold to the Lord Jesus Christ for the price of his blood!" As a result we become Jesus' purchased possession and must live for him rather than for ourselves, as Paul and Peter so clearly indicate.

The great preacher and biblical theologian John Calvin said precisely, "We are redeemed by the Lord for the purpose of consecrating ourselves and all our members to him."[2]

We need to notice one more thing before going on to the next point. Remember that we are in the application or "consequences" section of Romans. Redemption was introduced earlier in the letter, in Romans 3 (v. 24). So what we are finding here is an example of what I wrote in the last study: that doctrine is practical, and that practical material must be doctrinal if it is to be of any help at all. We *are* dealing with a practical matter here, namely, "How should we then live?" But the very first thing to be said in explaining how we should live is the meaning and implication of redemption. In other words, we cannot have true Christian living without the gospel.

Death to Our Past

Redemption from sin through Christ is not the only doctrine the Christian life of self-sacrifice is built on, however. A second doctrine is our having died to the past by having become new creatures in Christ, if we are truly converted. In Romans 6 Paul argued, much as he is going to do in Romans 12, that because we have "died to sin" we are unable to "live in it any longer" (v. 2). Therefore, instead of offering the parts of our bodies "to sin, as instruments of wickedness," as we used to do, we must instead offer ourselves "to God, as those who have been brought from death to life," and offer the parts of our bodies to him "as instruments of righteousness" (v. 13).

Having "died to sin" does not mean that we have become unresponsive to sin or that we should die to it or that we are dying to it day by day or that we have died to sin's guilt. Here the verb *die* is an aorist, which refers to something that has been done once for all, and what it refers to is the change that has come about as a result of our being saved. The sentence "we died to sin" means that as a result of our union with Jesus Christ by the work of the Holy Spirit, we have become new creatures in Christ so that we can never go back to being what we were. We are to start the Christian life with that knowledge, knowing that we cannot go back and that, if we cannot go back, there is no other direction for us to go but forward.

Let me review this teaching by summarizing what I wrote in my study of Romans 6:11 in the second volume of my detailed studies of that book.[3] I said that dying to sin does *not* mean:

1. That it is my duty to die to sin.
2. That I am commanded to die to sin.
3. That I am to consider sin as a dead force within me.
4. That sin in me has been eradicated.
5. That I am dead to sin so long as I am gaining mastery over it.
6. That counting myself dead to sin makes me insensitive to it.

What Paul is saying is that we have already died to sin in the sense that we cannot successfully return to our old lives. Therefore, since that is true, we might as well get on with the task of living for the Lord Jesus Christ as Christians. In other words, we need to forget about sinning and instead present our bodies as "living sacrifices" to God.

Dying to Live

The third point about what it means to "live by dying" is the paradox itself, namely, that it is by dying to our own desires in order to serve Christ that we actually learn to live.

I do not think there is any difficulty in understanding what this means. We understand only too well that dying to self means putting personal desires behind us in order to put first (1) the desires of God for us and (2) the needs of other people. And we understand the underlying promise, too. The promise is that if we do this, we will experience a full and rewarding life. We will be happy Christians. The problem here is not with our understanding. The problem is that we do not believe it. Or, if we do believe it in a general way, we at least do not believe it in regard to ourselves. We think that if we deny ourselves, we will be miserable. Yet this is nothing less than disbelieving God. It is a failure of faith.

So I ask, Whom are you willing to believe? Yourself, reinforced by the world and its way of thinking? Or Jesus Christ?

I say "Jesus" specifically, because I want to remind you of his teaching from the beginning of the Sermon on the Mount. He speaks there about how to be happy. Indeed, the adjective he uses is even stronger than that. It is the powerful word *blessed,* meaning "to be favored by God." Jesus said,

> Blessed are the poor in spirit,
>   for theirs is the kingdom of heaven.
> Blessed are those who mourn,
>   for they will be comforted.
> Blessed are the meek,
>   for they will inherit the earth.
> Blessed are those who hunger and thirst for
>   righteousness,
>   for they will be filled.
> Blessed are the merciful,
>   for they will be shown mercy.
> Blessed are the pure in heart,
>   for they will see God.
> Blessed are the peacemakers,
>   for they will be called sons of God.

Blessed are those who are persecuted because of
    righteousness,
  for theirs is the kingdom of heaven.

Matthew 5:3–10

We call these statements the Beatitudes—the way to
happiness or blessing. But this is not the way the world
thinks one finds happiness. If a director of one of today's
popular television sit-coms or the editor of a widely cir-
culating fashion magazine were to rewrite the Beatitudes
from a contemporary point of view, I suppose they would
go like this: "Blessed are the rich, for they can have all
they want; blessed are the powerful, for they can control others; blessed are the sexually liberated, for they
can fully satisfy themselves; blessed are the famous,
because they are envied." Isn't that the world's way, the
way of life toward which even Christians instinctively
incline, rather than the way of sacrifice?

But think it through carefully. Although the world
promises blessings for those who follow these standards,
is this what they find? Do they actually find happiness?

Consider a person who thinks that the way to happiness is wealth. He sets his heart on stockpiling $100,000.
He gets it, but he is not happy. He raises his goal to
$200,000. When he gets that and is still unhappy, he tries
to accumulate a million dollars, but happiness eludes
him. John D. Rockefeller, one of the richest men in the
world in his day, was asked on one occasion, "How much
money is enough?"

He was honest enough to answer wryly, "Just a little
bit more."

A Texas millionaire once said, "I thought money could
buy happiness. I have been miserably disillusioned."

Another person thinks he will find happiness through
controlling others, so he goes into politics, where he

thinks the key to power lies. He runs for a local election and wins. After that he sets his sights on a congressional seat, then on a place in the Senate. If he is talented enough and the circumstances are favorable, he may even hope to be President. But power never satisfies. One of the world's great statesmen once told Billy Graham, "I am an old man. Life has lost all meaning. I am ready to take a fateful leap into the unknown."

Still another person tries the path of sexual liberation. She launches into the swinging-singles scene where the average week consists of "happy hours," Friday-night parties, weekend overnight escapes into the country, and a rapid exchange of partners. But it does not work. Several years ago, CBS did a television documentary on the singles lifestyle in Southern California, interviewing about half a dozen women. They all said roughly the same thing: "We were told that this was the fun way to live, but all the men want to do is get in bed with you. We have had enough of that to last a lifetime."

Does the world's "me first" philosophy lead to happiness? Is personal indulgence the answer? You do not have to be a genius to see through that facade. It is an empty promise. Paul calls it "a lie" (Rom. 1:25).

So wake up, Christian. Listen to Paul when he pleads, "Therefore, I urge you, brothers, in view of God's mercy, to offer your bodies as living sacrifices, holy and pleasing to God—this is your spiritual act of worship. Do not conform any longer to the pattern of this world, but be transformed by the renewing of your mind. Then you will be able to test and approve what God's will is—his good, pleasing and perfect will."

God does not lie. His Word is utterly reliable. You will find his way to be "good, pleasing and perfect" if you will bend to it.

The Victim and the Priest

And that brings us to the fourth and final point about the Christian life. The first two points concerned what God has done for us in redeeming us and joining us to Jesus Christ by the Holy Spirit so that we become new creatures. The third point was the apparent paradox: life-by-dying. This last point is neither something that has been done for us nor even a mere paradoxical statement. It is an urgent appeal to us to do something: to offer ourselves as living sacrifices to God. This cannot be done for us. It is something we ourselves must do.

May I put it in other terms? It is the "obedience that comes from faith," which Paul wrote about early in Romans, saying, "Through him and for his name's sake, we received grace and apostleship to call people from among all the Gentiles to the obedience that comes from faith" (Rom. 1:5). So you see, again we are back to one of the great doctrinal teachings offered earlier.

What an interesting mental picture Paul creates for us in Romans 12:1. A sacrifice is something offered to God by a priest. A priest would take a sacrifice brought by a worshiper, carry it to the altar, kill it, pour out the blood, and then burn the victim's body. In that procedure the priest and the offering were two separate entities. But in this arresting image of what it is to live a genuinely Christian life, Paul shows us that the priest and the offering are the same. Furthermore, we are the priests who present the offering, and the offering we present is our own bodies.

Is there a model for this in Scripture? Of course, there is. It is the model of Jesus himself, for he was both the sacrifice and the priest who made the sacrifice. We have a statement of this in one of our great communion hymns, translated from a sixth-century Latin text by the Scotsman Robert Campbell (in 1849). The first verse states,

> At the Lamb's high feast we sing
> Praise to our victorious King,
> Who hath washed us in the tide
> Flowing from his pierced side;
> Praise we him whose love divine
> Gives his sacred blood for wine,
> Gives his body for the feast,
> *Christ the Victim, Christ the Priest.*

I know there is an enormous difference between the sacrifice that Jesus made for us and our own sacrifices of ourselves. Jesus' sacrifice was an atoning sacrifice. He died in our place, bearing the punishment of God for our sin so that we might not have to bear it. His death was substitutionary. Our sacrifices are not at all like that. They are not an atonement for sin in any sense. But they are like Christ's sacrifice in this at least, that we are the ones who make them and that the sacrifices we offer are ourselves.

And we remember another distinction, too. In the Old Testament the priests made different kinds of sacrifices. There were sacrifices for sin, of course. These looked forward to the death of Jesus Christ and explained it as a substitutionary atonement. They were fulfilled by Jesus' death and are not repeatable. In this sense "we have been made holy through the sacrifice of the body of Jesus Christ *once for all,*" as the author of Hebrews says (Heb. 10:10). But in addition to the sacrifices for sin there were also what were called "sacrifices of thanksgiving," which were exactly what they sound like—sacrifices by worshipers who simply wanted to thank God for some great blessing or deliverance. It is this kind of sacrifice that we offer when we offer God ourselves.

Sacrifice?

What an utterly unpleasant word for our day! Today no one wants to be a sacrifice, if they ever did. In fact, people do not want to sacrifice even a single little thing. We want to acquire things instead. True. But this is where the Christian life starts, all the same. It is God's instruction and desire for us, and it is "good, pleasing and perfect" even if it does not seem to be that, now or ever.

Will you trust God that he knows what he is doing? Will you believe him in this as in other matters? If you believe him, you will do exactly what the apostle Paul urges you to do in Romans 12:1–2. You will offer your body as a "living sacrifice" to God and thereby prove that his will for you is indeed utterly "good, pleasing and perfect."

How to Be a Living Sacrifice

"holy and pleasing to God"

It is of the body that the apostle here speaks, and it is not proper to extract out of his language more than it contains. . . . This shows the importance of serving God with the body as well as with the soul.

Robert Haldane

Not long ago I reread parts of Charles Dickens' wonderful historical novel *A Tale of Two Cities.* The cities are Paris and London, of course, and the story is set in the years of the French Revolution, when thousands of innocent people were being executed on the guillotine by supporters of the revolution. As usual with Dickens' stories, the plot is complex, but it reaches a never-to-be-forgotten climax when Sydney Carton, a disreputable character in the story, substitutes himself for his friend Charles Darney, who was being held for execution in the Bastille. Darney, who has been condemned to die, goes free, and Carton goes to the scaffold for him, saying, "It is a far, far better thing I do, than I have ever done; it is a far, far better rest I go to, than I have ever known." The tale is so well written that it still moves me to tears when I read it, even though I have read it several times.

Few things move us to hushed awe so much as a person's sacrifice of his or her life for someone else. It is the ultimate proof of true love.

If we love Jesus, we are to sacrifice ourselves for him. Jesus said, "Greater love has no one than this, that he lay down his life for his friends" (John 15:13), and he did that for us. He did it literally. The self-sacrifice of Sydney Carton for his friend Darney is only a story, albeit a moving one, but Jesus actually died on the cross for our salvation. Now, because he loved us and gave himself for us, we who love him are likewise to give ourselves to him as "living sacrifices."

But there is a tremendous difference between Jesus' sacrifice and ours. As I said in the last study, Jesus died in our place, bearing the punishment of God for our sin so that we might not have to bear it. Our sacrifices are not at all like that. They are not an atonement for sin in any sense. But they are like Christ's in this at least, that we are the ones who make them and that the sacrifices we make are ourselves. It is what Paul is talking about when he writes, "Therefore, I urge you, brothers, in view of God's mercy, to offer your bodies as living sacrifices, holy and pleasing to God—this is your spiritual act of worship" (Rom. 12:1).

I have already introduced the matter of sacrifice. In this study I want to explore its nature a bit further, asking: What exactly is meant by it and how are we to do it?

Living Sacrifices

The first point is the obvious one: This is to be a living sacrifice rather than a dead one. That was quite a novel idea in Paul's day, of course, though we have lost this by becoming overly familiar with it.

In Paul's day, sacrifices were always killed. In Jewish religious practices particularly, the animal was brought to the priest, the sins of the person bringing the sacrifice were confessed over the animal, thereby transferring them to it symbolically. Then the animal was put to death. It was a vivid way of reminding everyone that "the wages of sin is death" (Rom. 6:23) and that the salvation of sinners is by substitution. In those sacrifices the animal died in place of the worshiper. It died so that the worshiper might not have to die. But now, with a burst of divinely inspired creativity, Paul reveals that the sacrifices we are to offer are to be *living,* not dead. We are to offer our lives to God so that, as a result, we might "no longer live for [ourselves] but for him who died for [us] and was raised again" (2 Cor. 5:15).

Living sacrifices, yes. But with what life? Certainly not our old sinful lives in which, when we lived in them, we were already dead. Rather, we offer the new spiritual lives that have been given to us by Christ.

Robert Smith Candlish was a Scottish pastor who lived over a hundred years ago (1806–1873) and who left us some marvelous studies of the Bible. One set of these studies is of Romans 12, and in it there is a paragraph in which he reflects on the nature of the life we are to offer God. "What life?" Candlish asks. "Not merely animal life, the life that is common to all sentient and moving creatures; not merely, in addition to that, intelligent life, the life that characterizes all beings capable of thought and voluntary choice; but spiritual life: life in the highest sense; the very life which those on whose behalf the sacrifice of atonement is presented lost, when they fell into that state which makes a sacrifice of atonement necessary."[1]

What this means, among other things, is that we must be believers if we are to give ourselves to God as he requires. Other people may give God their money or time or even take up a religious vocation, but only a Christian can give back to God that new spiritual life in Christ that he or she has first been given. Indeed, it is only *because* we have been made alive in Christ that we are able to do this or even want to.

Offering Our Bodies

The second thing we need to see about the nature of the sacrifice that God requires is that it involves the giving to God of our bodies. Some of the older commentators stress that offering our bodies really means to offer our total selves, all that we are. Calvin wrote, "By *bodies* he means not only our skin and bones, but the totality of which we are composed."[2] Although it is true that we are to offer God all that we are, most commentators today rightly refuse to pass over the word *bodies* quite this easily, because they recognize how much the Bible stresses the importance of our bodies.

For example, Leon Morris says, "Paul surely expected Christians to offer to God not only their bodies but their whole selves. . . . But we should bear in mind that the body is very important in the Christian understanding of things. Our bodies may be 'implements of righteousness' (6:13) and 'members of Christ' (1 Cor. 6:15). The body is a temple of the Holy Spirit (1 Cor. 6:19); Paul can speak of being 'holy both in body and in spirit' (1 Cor. 7:34). He knows that there are possibilities of evil in the body but that in the believer 'the body of sin' has been brought to nothing (6:6)."[3]

In a similar manner, Robert Haldane says, "It is of the body that the apostle here speaks, and it is not proper to extract out of his language more than it contains. . . . This shows the importance of serving God with the body as well as with the soul."[4]

Paul does not elaborate in Romans 12 upon what he means by presenting our bodies to God "as living sacrifices," but we are not left in the dark about his meaning since this is not a new idea, not even in Romans. It has already appeared in chapter 6. In that chapter Paul said, "Therefore do not let sin reign in your mortal body so that you obey its evil desires. Do not offer the parts of your body to sin, as instruments of wickedness, but rather offer yourselves to God, as those who have been brought from death to life; and offer the parts of your body to him as instruments of righteousness. For sin shall not be your master, because you are not under law, but under grace" (vv. 12–14). This is the point at which Paul first began to talk about sanctification, and the point he was making there is the same one he is making here, namely, that we are to serve God by offering him our bodies.

Sin can control us through our bodies, but this need not happen. So, rather than offering our bodies as instruments of sin, we are to offer God our bodies as instruments for doing his will. To be practical we need to think about this as involving specific parts of our bodies.

1. *Our minds.* I begin with the mind because, although we think of ourselves largely as our minds and thus separate our minds from our bodies, our minds actually are parts of our bodies and the victory we need to achieve begins here. In this study I will not say a great deal about

presenting our minds to God, because I will be treating this more fully later when I talk about mind renewal. But I remind you that this is the point at which Paul himself begins in verse 2: "Do not conform any longer to the pattern of this world, but be transformed by *the renewing of your mind*" (emphasis mine).

Have you ever considered that what you do with your mind will determine a great deal of what you will become as a Christian? If you fill your mind only with the products of our secular culture, you will remain secular and sinful. If you fill your head with trashy "pop" novels, you will begin to live like the trashy characters you read about. If you do little else but watch television, you will begin to act like the scoundrels on the screen. On the other hand, if you feed your mind on the Bible and Christian books, train it by godly conversation, and discipline it to critique what you see and hear by applying biblical truths to the world's ideas, you will grow in godliness and become increasingly useful to God.

For every secular book you read, make it your goal also to read one good Christian book, a book that can stretch your mind spiritually.

2. *Our eyes and ears.* The mind is not the only part of our body by which we receive and filter impressions and which must therefore be offered to God as an instrument of righteousness. We also receive impressions through our eyes and ears, and these, too, must be surrendered to God.

Sociologists tell us that by the age of twenty-one the average young person has been bombarded by 300,000 commercial messages, all arguing from the assumption that personal gratification is the dominant goal in life.[5] Our modern means of communication put the acquisition of "things" before godliness. In fact, they never mention godliness at all. How are you going to grow in godliness if you are constantly watching television or reading printed ads or listening to secular radio?

I am not advocating an evangelical monasticism in which we retreat from the culture, though it is far better to retreat from it than perish in it. But somehow the secular input must be counterbalanced by the spiritual. Another simple goal might be for you to spend as many hours studying your Bible, praying, and going to church as watching television.

3. *Our tongues.* The tongue is also part of our body, and what we do with it is important either for good or evil. James, the Lord's brother, wrote, "The tongue also is a fire, a world of evil among the parts of the body. It corrupts the whole person, sets the whole course of his life on fire, and is itself set on fire by hell" (James 3:6). If your tongue is not given to God as an instrument of righteousness in his hands, this will be true of you. You do not need to be a Hitler and plunge the world into armed conflict to do evil with your tongue. A little bit of gossip or slander will suffice.

What you need to do is use your tongue to praise and serve God. For one thing, you should learn how to recite Scripture with it. You probably know the words of many popular songs. Can you not also use your tongue to speak God's words? And how about worship? You should use your tongue to praise God by means of hymns and other Christian songs. Above all, you should use your tongue to witness to others about the person and work of Jesus Christ.

Here is another goal for you if you want to grow in godliness: Use your tongue as much to tell others about Jesus as for idle conversation.

4. *Our hands and feet.* There are several important biblical passages about our hands and feet. In 1 Thessalonians 4:11–12, Paul tells us to work with our hands so that we will be self-supporting and not have to rely on

others: "Make it your ambition to lead a quiet life, to mind your own business and to work with your hands, just as we told you, so that your daily life may win the respect of outsiders and so that you will not be dependent on anybody." In Ephesians 4:28, he tells us also to work so that we will have something to give to others who are in need: "He who has been stealing must steal no longer, but must work, doing something useful with his own hands, that he might have something to share with those in need."

As far as our feet are concerned, Paul wrote in Romans 10 of the need that others have for the gospel, saying, "How can they hear without someone preaching to them? And how can they preach unless they are sent? As it is written, 'How beautiful are the feet of those who bring good news!'" (Rom. 10:14–15).

What do you do with *your* hands? Where do *your* feet take you? Do you allow them to take you to where Christ is denied or blasphemed? To where sin is openly practiced? Are you spending most of your free time loitering in the "hot" singles clubs or in other unsavory places? You will not grow in godliness there. On the contrary, you will fall from righteous conduct. Instead, let your feet carry you into the company of those who love and serve God. Or, as you go into the world, let it be to serve the world and witness to it in Christ's name. Use your feet and hands for him.

For every special secular function you attend, determine to attend a Christian function also. And when you go to a secular function, do so as a witness by word and action for the Lord Jesus Christ.

Holiness, without Which . . .

The third word Paul uses to indicate the nature of the sacrifices we are to offer God is "holy." Any sacrifice we make must be holy. That is, it must be without spot or blemish and be consecrated entirely to God. Anything less is an insult to the great and holy God all people are to serve. But how much more must *we* be holy—we who have been purchased "not with perishable things such as silver or gold . . . but with the precious blood of Christ, a lamb without blemish or defect" (1 Peter 1:18–19). Peter explained, "But just as he who called you is holy, so be holy in all you do; for it is written: 'Be holy, because I am holy'" (vv. 15–16). The author of Hebrews said, "Without holiness no one will see the Lord" (Heb. 12:14).

This is the very heart of what we are talking about when we speak of living sacrifices, of course. Or, to put it in other language, holiness is the end of the matter. Or, to put it in still other language, it is the point to which the entire epistle of Romans has been heading. Romans is about salvation. But, as someone has wisely noted, salvation does not mean that Jesus died to save us *in* our sins but to save us *from* them.

Handley C. G. Moule expressed this well. "As we actually approach the rules of holiness now before us, let us once more recollect what we have seen all along in the Epistle, that holiness is the aim and issue of the entire Gospel. It is indeed an 'evidence of life,' infinitely weighty in the enquiry whether a man knows God indeed and is on the way to his heaven. But it is much more; it is the expression of life; it is the form and action in which life is intended to come out. . . . We who believe are 'chosen' and 'ordained' to 'bring forth fruit' (John 15:16), fruit much and lasting."[6]

Is there any subject that is more generally neglected among evangelicals in America in our day than holiness? I do not think so. Yet there was a time when holiness was a serious pursuit of anyone who called himself a Christian, and when how one lived and what one was inside was vitally important.

England's J. I. Packer has written a book called *Redis-covering Holiness* in which he calls attention to this matter. "The Puritans insisted that all life and relationships must become 'holiness to the Lord.' John Wesley told the world that God had raised up methodism 'to spread scriptural holiness throughout the land.' Phoebe Palmer, Handley Moule, Andrew Murray, Jessie Penn-Lewis, F. B. Meyer, Oswald Chambers, Horatius Bonar, Amy Carmichael, and L. B. Maxwell are only a few of the leading figures in the 'holiness revival' that touched all evangelical Christendom between the mid-nineteenth and mid-twentieth centuries."[7]

But today? In our time, holiness is largely forgotten as an important quality for Christians. So we do not try to be holy. We hardly know what it means. And we do not look for holiness in others. The great parish minister and revival preacher Robert Murray McCheyne once said, "My people's greatest need is my personal holiness." But what pulpit committees look for holiness in a new pastor today? Hardly any. They look for a winsome personality, good communication skills, administrative ability, and other secular things.

As for ourselves, we do not seek out books or tapes on holiness or attend seminars designed to draw us closer to God. We want information on "How to Be Happy," "How to Raise Children," "How to Have a Good Sex Life," "How to Succeed in Business," and so on.

Fortunately, this lack has begun to be noticed by some evangelical leaders who are disturbed by it and have begun to address the subject. I commend Packer's book, as well as a book written a few years ago by Jerry Bridges called *The Pursuit of Holiness*. There is also the older classic by the English Bishop John Charles Ryle on the same topic.[8]

"Pleasing to God"

The final words that Paul uses to describe the nature of our living sacrifices is "pleasing to God." But this is also a conclusion for what I have been saying so far in this study, since the point is that if we do what Paul has urged us to do—namely, to offer our "bodies as living sacrifices, holy . . . to God"—we will also find that what we have done is pleasing to him, or acceptable.

It is amazing to me that God could find anything we might be able to do to be pleasing. But it is so! Notice that the word *pleasing* occurs twice in this short paragraph. The first time, which is what we are looking at here, it indicates that our offering of ourselves to God pleases him. The second time, which occurs at the end of verse 2, it indicates that when we do this we will find God's will for our lives to be pleasing as well as good and perfect. I understand that God's will for me should be pleasing—pleasing to me, that is. How could it be otherwise if God is an all-wise and all-good God? He must will what is good for me. But that my offering of myself to him should somehow also please *him*—when I know myself to be sinful and ignorant and halfhearted even in my best efforts—that is astonishing.

But so it is! The Bible tells me that at my best I am to think of myself as an "unworthy" servant (Luke 17:10). But it also says that if I live for Jesus, offering back to him what he has first given to me, then one day I will hear him say, "Well done, good and faithful servant! . . . Come and share your master's happiness!" (Matt. 25:21, 23).

Amazing Grace

"in view of *God's mercy*"

The secular world never understands Christian motivation. . . . From the plan of salvation I learn that the true driving force in authentic Christian living is, and ever must be, not the hope of gain, but the heart of gratitude.

J. I. Packer

What is it that motivates people to achieve all they are capable of achieving, or to be "the best they can be," as the army's recruitment ads have it? There are a number of possible answers.

One way to motivate people is to challenge them. Dale Carnegie, the author of *How to Win Friends and Influence People,* tells of a mill manager whose workers were not producing. The owner was named Charles Schwab, and he asked the manager what was wrong. "I have no idea," he said. "I've coaxed the men; I've pushed them; I've sworn and cussed; I've threatened them with damnation and being fired. Nothing works. They just won't produce."

"How many castings did your shift make today?" Schwab asked.

"Six."

Without saying anything else, Schwab picked up a piece of chalk and wrote a big number "6" on the floor. Then he walked away.

When the night shift came in, they saw the "6" and asked what it meant. "The big boss was here today," someone said. "He asked how many castings the day shift made, and we told him six. He chalked it on the floor."

The next morning Schwab walked through the mill again. The night shift had rubbed out the "6" and replaced it with an even bigger "7." When the day shift reported the next day they saw the "7." So the night shift thought it was better than the day shift, did it? They'd show them. So they pitched in furiously, and before they had left that evening they had rubbed out the "7" and replaced it with a "10." Schwab had increased production 66 percent in just twenty-four hours, simply by throwing down a challenge.[1]

Napoleon, the famous French general, said that men are moved by trinkets. He was referring to medals, and he meant that soldiers would risk even death for recognition.

Winston Churchill, the great statesman and prime minister of England during the hard days of the Second World War, motivated the British people by his vision of victory and his brilliant speeches. We can remember some of his words even today: "Victory—victory at all costs, victory in spite of all terror; victory however long

and hard the road may be." Churchill did not promise
the English people an easy time but rather "blood, toil,
tears and sweat." When they responded with their best
efforts, he dubbed it "their finest hour."

Moved by Mercy

But what is it that motivates Christians to live a Christian life? Or to use Paul's language in Romans 12:1, what
is it that motivates them to offer their bodies as living
sacrifices to God?

If you and I were as rational as we think we are and
sometimes claim to be, we would not need any encour-
agement to offer our bodies to God as living sacrifices,
because it would be the most reasonable thing in the
world for us to do. God is our Creator. He has redeemed
us from sin by the death of Jesus Christ. He has made us
alive in Christ. He loves us and cares for us. It is reasonable to love God and serve him in return for all he
has done for us. But we are not as rational as that, and
we do need urging, which is why Paul writes as he does
in Romans 12. In verse 1 Paul urges us to offer our bodies to God as living sacrifices, and the motivation he provides is God's mercy—"Therefore, I urge you, brothers,
in view of God's mercy, to offer your bodies as living sacrifices, holy and pleasing to God—this is your spiritual
act of worship" (emphasis mine).

Romans 12:1 is an amazing verse. It is one of those
portions of the Bible that is literally packed with meaning, which is why I have been trying to unpack it carefully in these studies.

We began by examining the word *therefore,* which
links the exhortation of Romans 12:1–2 to everything that
Paul has already written about in the letter. Next we
looked at the idea of *sacrifice,* finding that in genuine
Christianity we live by dying to self, as strange as that

may seem. Third, we explored the *nature of these sacri-fices,* seeing that (1) they are to be living not dead; (2) they involve giving the specific individual parts of our bodies to God for his service; (3) they must be holy; and (4) if they are these things, they will be acceptable to God.

But *why* should we present our bodies as living sac-rifices? That is the question I am raising now, and the answer, as I have already pointed out, is "in view of [or because of] God's mercy." In the Greek text the word *mercy* is plural rather than singular, as the New Inter-national Version has it, so the reason for giving ourselves to God is literally because of God's manifold mercies, that is, because he has been good to us in many ways.

This is entirely different from the way the world looks at things. Assuming that the world should ever get as far as being concerned about righteous living—and today it seems very doubtful that it could—the world would probably say: "The reason to live a moral life is that you are going to get in trouble if you don't." Or to give secu-lar thinking the greatest possible credit, perhaps it might say: "Because it is good for you."

That is not what we have here in Romans 12:1.

In *Rediscovering Holiness* J. I. Packer says, "The sec-ular world never understands Christian motivation. Faced with the question of what makes Christians tick, unbelievers maintain that Christianity is practiced only out of self-serving purposes. They see Christians as fear-ing the consequences of not being Christians (religion as fire insurance), or feeling the need of help and support to achieve their goals (religion as a crutch), or wishing to sustain a social identity (religion as a badge of respectability). No doubt all these motivations can be found among the membership of churches: it would be futile to dispute that. But just as a horse brought into a house is not thereby made human, so a self-seeking moti-vation brought into the church is not thereby made Christian, nor will holiness ever be the right name for religious routines thus motivated. From the plan of salvation I learn that the true driving force in authentic Christian living is, and ever must be, not the hope of gain, but the heart of gratitude."[2]

And, of course, that is exactly what Paul is teaching. As John Calvin wrote, "Paul's entreaty teaches us that men will never worship God with a sincere heart, or be roused to fear and obey him with sufficient zeal, until they properly understand how much they are indebted to his mercy."[3]

What Is Mercy?

"Mercy" is one of three words that are often found together in the Bible: goodness, grace, and mercy. "Goodness" is the most general term, involving all that emanates from God: his decrees, his creation, his laws, his providences. It extends to the elect and to the non-elect, though not in the same way. God is good, and everything he does is good. "Grace" denotes favor, particularly toward the undeserving. There is "common grace," the kind of favor God shows to all persons in that he sends rain on the just and unjust alike. There is also "special grace" or "saving grace," which is what he shows to those he is saving from their sins. "Mercy" is an aspect of grace, but the unique quality of mercy is that it is given to the pitiful.

Arthur W. Pink says, "Mercy . . . denotes the ready inclination of God to relieve the misery of fallen creatures. Thus 'mercy' presupposes sin."[4]

Let me show how this works by three examples.

"In the Beginning"

The first example is Adam. I would like you to try to put yourself in Adam's position at the very beginning of

human history and imagine how he must have felt when
God came to him in the Garden of Eden after he and Eve
had sinned by eating from the forbidden tree. You will
remember that God had warned Adam about eating, saying, "You are free to eat from any tree in the garden; but
you must not eat from the tree of the knowledge of good
and evil, for when you eat of it you will surely die" (Gen.
2:16–17). The Hebrew text actually says, "*On the day* you
eat of it you will die." But Adam and Eve had eaten of it,
and now God had come to them to demand an account-
ing (Gen. 3:9–13) and pronounce judgment (vv. 14–19).

"Where are you?" God called.

Adam and his wife had hidden among the trees when
they heard God coming, and they were terrified. God had
said they would die on the day they ate of the forbidden
tree. Eve must have expected to die. Adam must have
expected to die. "I heard you in the garden, and I was
afraid because I was naked; so I hid," Adam said.

"Who told you that you were naked?" God asked.
"Have you eaten from the tree that I commanded you not
to eat from?"

Adam confessed that he had eaten, though he blamed
the woman for getting him to do it.

God addressed the woman: "What is this you have
done?"

Eve blamed the serpent.

At last God began his judgments, beginning with the
serpent:

> Cursed are you above all the livestock
>   and all the wild animals!
> You will crawl on your belly
>   and you will eat dust
>   all the days of your life.
> And I will put enmity
>   between you and the woman,

and between your offspring and hers;
he will crush your head,
    and you will strike his heel (vv. 14–15).

God spoke to Eve next, foretelling pain in childbirth and a harsh struggle within the marriage. We call it the "battle of the sexes."

Finally, God addressed Adam:

Cursed is the ground because of you;
    through painful toil you will eat of it
    all the days of your life.
It will produce thorns and thistles for you,
    and you will eat the plants of the field.
By the sweat of your brow
    you will eat your food
until you return to the ground,
    since from it you were taken;
for dust you are
    and to dust you will return (vv. 17–19).

Imagine yourself in Adam's place, living through what I have described. God had told Adam and Eve that they would die, but they had not died. There had been judgments, of course. Sin always has consequences. But they had not been struck down. In fact, God had even announced the coming of a redeemer who one day would crush Satan's head and undo his work. Even more, God had illustrated the nature of Christ's atonement by killing animals, the innocent dying for the guilty, and then by clothing Adam and Eve with the animals' skins (v. 21). This was a picture of imputed righteousness.

How must Adam have felt? You do not need a theological degree to answer that. Adam must have been overwhelmed by an awareness of God's mercy. Adam deserved to die. But instead of killing him, God spared him and promised a savior instead.

No wonder Adam then named his wife "Eve," meaning "life-giver" or "mother." It was his way of express-
ing faith in God's promise, for God had said that it was
from the seed of the woman that the redeemer would
come. The memory of God's mercy must have kept Adam
looking to God in faith and living for God by faith
through his long life from that time forward, for Adam
lived a total of 930 years and fathered the line of godly
patriarchs that extended from him through his third son,
Seth, to Noah.

"The Worst of Sinners"

Here is my second example, this one from the New
Testament. It is Paul himself. In his earlier days, Paul
was called Saul. He was a fierce opponent of Christianity.
He was a Pharisee, the strictest sect of the Jews, and he
was zealous for the traditions of his fathers. This led him
to participate in the martyrdom of Stephen, and he followed that by arresting and otherwise persecuting many
of the early Christians. Having done what he could in
Jerusalem, Saul obtained letters to the leaders of the syn-
agogues in Damascus and went there to arrest any Christians he could find and carry them off to Jerusalem for
trial and possible death. Acts 9:3–15 tells us what happened next.

On the way, Jesus stopped Saul. There was a bright
light from heaven, and when Saul fell to the ground,
blinded by the light, he heard a voice speaking to him.
"Saul, Saul, why do you persecute me?"

"Who are you, Lord?" Saul asked.

"I am Jesus, whom you are persecuting," the voice
replied.

At this point Saul/Paul must have had feelings similar to those of Adam when God had appeared to him in
the Garden of Eden. True, God had not told Paul that he
would die if he persecuted Christians. He was perse-

cuting them in ignorance, supposing that he was serv-ing God. But he had been terribly mistaken. He had done great harm and had even participated in the killing of God's disciple Stephen. In that first moment of Paul's dawning apprehension, when he recognized that it was Jesus of Nazareth who was speaking to him, he must have thought that Jesus had appeared to him to judge him. He certainly deserved it. He must have expected to have been struck down and have died.

Instead Jesus had the blinded Paul led to Damascus, where he would be told what he should do. When the message came to him by a disciple named Ananias, it was that he was to be God's "chosen instrument to carry [the Lord's] name before the Gentiles and their kings and before the people of Israel" (Acts 9:15). Paul's eyes were opened.

Mercy? I should say it was. Paul never forgot it.

That is why, years later, he could write to his young friend and co-worker Timothy, saying, "Here is a trust-worthy saying that deserves full acceptance: Christ Jesus came into the world to save sinners—of whom I am the worst. But for that very reason I was shown mercy so that in me, the worst of sinners, Christ Jesus might dis-play his unlimited patience as an example for those who would believe on him and receive eternal life" (1 Tim. 1:15–16). It was because he knew himself to be a sinner saved only by the mercy and grace of God that Paul joy-fully gave himself to God as a living sacrifice and worked tirelessly to please him.

"A Slave of Slaves"

My third example is John Newton, an Englishman who lived from 1725 to 1807. Newton ran away to sea as a young boy and eventually went to Africa to participate in the slave trade. His reason for going, as he later wrote in his autobiography, was that he might "sin his fill."

And sin he did! But the path of sin is downhill, and Newton's path descended so low that he was eventually reduced to the position of a slave in his master's African compound. This man dealt in slaves, and while he was off on slaving expeditions Newton fell into the hands of the slave trader's African wife, who hated white men and vented her venom on Newton. Newton was forced to eat his food off the dusty floor like a dog, and at one point he was actually placed in chains. Sick and emaciated, he nearly died.

Newton escaped from this form of his slavery eventually. But he was still chained to sin and again went to sea, transporting slaves from the west coast of Africa to the New World. It was on his return from one of these slave voyages that Newton was wondrously converted.

The ship was overtaken by a fierce storm in the North Atlantic and was nearly sinking. The rigging was destroyed, water was pouring in. The seamen tried to seal the many leaks and brace the siding. Newton was sent down into the hold to pump water. He pumped for days, certain that the ship would sink and that he would be taken under with it and be drowned. But as he pumped water in the hold of that ship, God brought to Newton's mind some verses he had learned from his mother as a child, and they led to his conversion. The ship survived the storm. The sailors were saved. And sometime later, after Newton had left the slave trade, this former "slave of slaves" studied for the Christian ministry and finally became a great preacher. He even preached before the queen.

What was Newton's motivation? It was a profound awareness of the grace and mercy of God toward him, a wretched sinner. Newton wrote,

> Amazing grace—how sweet the sound—
> That saved a wretch like me!

I once was lost, but now am found,
Was blind, but now I see.

Newton never forgot God's mercy to him. Once a friend of Newton's was complaining about someone who was resistant to the gospel and living a life of great sin. "Sometimes I almost despair of that man," the friend remarked.

"I never did despair of any man since God saved me," said Newton.

In his most advanced years Newton's mind began to fail and he had to stop preaching. But when friends came to visit him he frequently remarked, "I am an old man. My mind is almost gone. But I can remember two things: I am a great sinner, and Jesus is a great Savior." Certainly the mercy of God moved Newton to offer his body as a living sacrifice to God and to seek to please him.

Love So Amazing

Now I come to *you*. Up to this point I have been asking you to put yourself in the places of Adam and Paul and John Newton, trying to feel what they must have felt as an awareness of the greatness of the mercy of God swept over them. If you are a Christian, you should be feeling the same things yourself, even without reference to Adam or Paul or other such characters.

Ephesians 2 describes your experience. It says that before God revealed his mercy to you, you were "dead in your transgressions and sins" (v. 1). You "followed the ways of this world and of the ruler of the kingdom of the air" (v. 2) and were "by nature" an object of God's "wrath" (v. 3). "You were separate from Christ, excluded from citizenship in Israel" and a foreigner "to the covenants of the promise, without hope and without God in the world" (v. 12). That was once your condition.

But now listen to what God did.

"Because of his great love for us, God, who is rich in mercy, made us alive with Christ even when we were dead in transgressions—it is by grace you have been saved. And God raised us up with Christ and seated us with him in the heavenly realms in Christ Jesus, in order that in the coming ages he might show the incomparable riches of his grace, expressed in his kindness to us in Christ Jesus" (Eph. 2:4–7).

That is the nature of the goodness, love, grace, and mercy of our great God. If you are a Christian, shouldn't it motivate you to the most complete offer of your body to him as a living sacrifice and to the highest possible level of obedience and service? How can it do otherwise? In my opinion, you can never understand and accurately appreciate what God has done in showing you mercy in Christ without replying wholeheartedly,

> Love so amazing, so divine,
> Demands my soul, my life, my all.

Service That Makes Sense

"this is *your spiritual act of worship*"

. . . we are not "spiritual" in the biblical sense except as the use of our bodies is characterized by conscious, intelligent, consecrated devotion to the service of God.

John Murray

We come now to the last phrase of Romans 12:1, "this is your spiritual act of worship," or, as the King James Version has it, "which is your reasonable service." I want to begin by saying something that I know will be disturbing to some people. The Greek words are ambiguous. That is, they admit of more than one translation.

Once I was in California speaking on "Limited [or Definite] Atonement." After I had defined and defended this doctrine, I began to deal with verses that seem to teach the opposite. One of these is 2 Peter 3:9, which says, "The Lord is not slow in keeping his promise, as some understand slowness. He is patient with you, not wanting anyone to perish, but everyone to come to repentance." I gave my understanding of this verse, which is that Peter is not speaking of all people in this passage but of the elect, his point being that God has not yet brought the final judgment but, rather, is delaying it so that the full number of the elect might be born, come to faith in Jesus Christ, and live for him.

A woman at this conference was disturbed by my message and puzzled by my interpretation of this verse. She asked one of the other speakers about it. Then she became even more disturbed, because he gave her a different explanation. Although the other speaker affirmed what I had been teaching about definite atonement, he felt that 2 Peter 3:9 is to be explained by the different ways we use the word *will*. One way is to refer to God's efficacious will, according to which things happen precisely because God *wills* them. The other is to refer only to God's natural but not necessarily efficacious disposition. He felt that Peter uses the word this way, meaning only that God does not enjoy punishing people.

When this woman spoke to me about it afterward, she was greatly agitated to know that two Bible teachers could have two different interpretations of such a key verse, and she walked away angrily and in turmoil.

What Is the Meaning?

Unfortunately, there are two different ways in which the idea of spiritual worship in Romans 12:1 may be understood. The Greek noun translated "worship" is

latreia, which can mean either "service" or "worship,"
which is not too puzzling since worship of God can easily be understood to be service. The plural of *latreia* can
even mean "rites" or "duties." However, the adjective in
this important combination of words is *logikos,* which
can mean either "spiritual" or "rational," and when it is
coupled to the noun two rather different meanings are
possible, as I said.

The older meaning is preserved in the well-known
translation of the King James Bible: "your reasonable service." The newer meaning is "your spiritual act of worship," which is what we have in the New International
Version.

What is it? Is it "reasonable service"? Or is it "spiritual worship"? One answer is that the Greek words may
actually embrace both ideas at the same time, spiritual
worship being thought of also as rational service. But if
I am forced to make a choice, I find myself siding with
John Murray, who notes rightly that "reasonable or rational is a more literal rendering."[1] *Logikos* has given us
the English word "logical," which means reasonable or
according to reason, and this should also be the preferred
meaning, if for no other reason than that in the next verse
Paul talks about mind renewal.

So Paul really is talking about something reasonable,
saying that the living sacrifice that he is urging upon us
here is logical.

Even more, the service itself is to be performed rea-
sonably, or with the mind. We are going to look at that
again, but here is the way Murray expands the idea: "The
service here in view is worshipful service and the apostle characterizes it as 'rational' because it is worship that
derives its character as acceptable to God from the fact
that it enlists our mind, our reason, our intellect. It is
rational in contrast with what is mechanical or auto-
matic. . . . The lesson to be derived from the term 'ra-

tional' is that we are not 'spiritual' in the biblical sense
except as the use of our bodies is characterized by conscious, intelligent, consecrated devotion to the service
of God."[2]

To understand these words well we must comprehend
two things. First, we must understand the kind of service that is required. Second, we need to see why such
demanding service is so reasonable.

Giving God Ourselves

As far as the first of these two matters is concerned,
we have already spent a good bit of time exploring what
this kind of service is about. It concerns what Paul calls
"sacrifice," and we saw that sacrifice itself involves several things. First, it must be a *living* sacrifice. That is,
our lives are to be given to God in active and continuing service. Second, it involves the offering of our *bodies.* In other words, we must give God the use of our
minds, eyes, ears, tongues, hands, feet, and other body
parts. Third, we must be *holy.* Moreover, we saw that if
we do all this, the sacrifices we make to God will be
pleasing to him.

Our problem, of course, is that we do not want to give
God ourselves. True, we will give him some of our possessions. It is relatively easy to give God money, though
even here we are frequently far less than generous. We
will even give God a certain amount of our time. We will
volunteer for charitable work or serve on church committees. But we will not truly give ourselves to God. Yet
without *ourselves,* these other "gifts" mean nothing to
the Almighty.

Let me say that you will only begin to understand the
Christian life when you realize that God does not want
your money or your time without yourself. You are the
one for whom Jesus died. You are the one he loves. So

when the Bible speaks of reasonable service, as it does here, it means that *you* are what God wants. It is sad if you try to substitute things and time for that, the greatest gift.

In the Old Testament there is a wonderful illustration of how we sometimes substitute things for ourselves. It is the story of Jacob's return to his own country as related in Genesis 32. Jacob had cheated his brother Esau out of his father Isaac's blessing about twenty years before, and he had been forced to run away because his brother was threatening to kill him. Twenty years is a long time. Over those two decades Jacob had gradually forgotten his brother's threats. But when it came time to go home, which is what this chapter describes, Jacob began to remember the past and grew increasingly fearful of what might happen.

Moving along toward Canaan with Laban behind him and his own country in front of him, Jacob had time to think. He remembered his own disreputable conduct. He recollected Esau's murderous threats. Every step became more difficult. Finally, when he came to the brook Jabbok that marked the border of his brother's territory, he looked across to where Esau lived and was terrified. If Jacob could have gone back, he would have. But there was no way to go except forward.

What was he to do?

The first thing he did was send some servants ahead to see if they could find Esau and perhaps get a feeling for what he was planning to do. They had not gone very far, when they ran into Esau, who was actually coming to meet Jacob. Unfortunately, he had four hundred men with him. This was a huge army from Jacob's point of view, and he could only assume the worst, namely, that Esau was coming to kill him. He thought quickly, then divided his family, servants, and flocks into two groups, reasoning that if Esau attacked one group, the other might escape.

Ah, but what if Jacob was in the group that Esau attacked?

On second thought that didn't seem to be a very good plan. So Jacob backed up and tried something else. He decided to appease his brother with gifts. First he sent him a present of two hundred female goats. He sent a servant along to drive the herd and gave the servant these instructions: "When my brother Esau meets you and asks, 'To whom do you belong, and where are you going, and who owns all these animals in front of you?' then you are to say, 'They belong to your servant Jacob. They are a gift to my lord Esau, and he is coming behind us'" (Gen. 32:17–18).

After this, Jacob sent a group of twenty male goats, and he gave the servant in charge of this flock the same message. Say, "They belong to your servant Jacob. They are a gift to my lord Esau, and he is coming behind us."

But what if Esau was not satisfied with the goats? What if he had all the goats he wanted? Jacob decided to send two hundred ewes, then twenty rams. After this, he sent over the rest of his livestock: "thirty female camels with their young, forty cows and ten bulls, and twenty female donkeys and ten male donkeys" (v. 15). Each group had Jacob's servants in charge, and to each servant he gave the same message. It must have been an amusing picture—all Jacob's possessions stretched out across the desert going toward Esau.

But there was more. After he had sent the animals, Jacob sent his least-favored wife, Leah, and her children across the Jabbok, followed by his favorite wife, Rachel, with her children. Then he sent over everything else he had. Finally, there at last, all alone and trembling, was Jacob.

I suppose that if he had known the chorus, he might have been singing, "I surrender all." All the goats, that is. All the sheep. All the camels. All the cows. All the bulls. All the donkeys. He had given up everything, but he had still not given himself. That is what some of us do with God. We tell God that we will give him time, so we volunteer to help with something around the church. We give him some money, too. But we do not give ourselves.

That night at the Jabbok, God came in the form of an angel and wrestled with Jacob to bring him to the point of personal submission, after which this scheming, stiff-necked man was reborn. At least he was never the same again. When is the angel going to come and wrestle with you? Does he need to?

Why Is Our Service Reasonable?

Let's not wait for the angel, however. Let's deal with this matter of sacrificial service to God now, and let's do it by moving on to the second half of what this study is about. Let's ask why such demanding service is so "reasonable." Why is it reasonable to serve God sacrificially? Here are five reasons.

1. *It is reasonable because of what God has already done for us.* We touched on this point in the first of our studies of Romans 12:1–2, because it is implied in the word with which Paul begins this final major section of the letter: "therefore." We saw that "therefore" refers back to everything Paul said earlier, when he discussed our need as sinners who are under the wrath of God, on a destructive downhill path, and unable to help ourselves. Paul has also shown that we are not even inclined to help ourselves. Instead of drawing close to God, who is our only hope, we run away from him, suppressing

even the truths about God known from the revelation of himself in nature.

Yet God has not let it go at that. God has intervened to save us by the work of Jesus Christ, who died for us, and by the inner work of the Holy Spirit, who enables us to understand what Jesus has accomplished, to repent of our sin, and to trust him for our salvation. Then God has also joined us to Jesus Christ to make us different people from what we were before.

Paul expounded that and more in the letter's first eleven chapters. So now, when he gets to chapter 12, he says, "Look what God has done. Is it not reasonable to give yourself utterly and sacrificially to a God who has given himself utterly and sacrificially for you?"

Let me make that personal. Are you a believer in Jesus Christ? Are you trusting him for your salvation? Has the Holy Spirit made you alive in Jesus Christ? If he has, what can be more reasonable than to give yourself to him? What is more logical than to serve God wholeheartedly in this way?

2. *It is reasonable because of what God is continuing to do.* The salvation of a Christian is not just a past event. It is also a present experience, because God is continuing to work in those whom he has brought to faith in Jesus Christ. It is difficult to make changes in our lives, break destructive habits, form new ways of thinking, and thereby please God. But this is exactly what God is doing in us. It is what this text is about. God does not start a project and abandon it. When God starts something, he always brings it to completion. He is doing this with you. Therefore, it is absurd to oppose his purposes. It is futile. The only reasonable thing is to join God and get on with what he is leading you to do.

3. *It is reasonable because such service is God's will for us, and his is a good, pleasing, and perfect will.* This point anticipates Romans 12:2, which we are also going

to study in detail, as we have verse 1. Verse 2 says, "Do not conform any longer to the pattern of this world, but be transformed by the renewing of your mind. Then you will be able to test and approve what God's will is—his good, pleasing and perfect will."

Christians often get greatly hung up on the idea of discovering what God's specific will is for their lives. In my judgment, there clearly are specific plans for our lives that God has determined in advance, because he has predetermined all things. The difficulty is that he has not revealed (and does not usually reveal) those specifics to us. They are part of the hidden wisdom and counsels of God, and they are not known by us simply because they *are* hidden. But although these details are not made known, general but very important things are, and the most important of these general things is that God wants us to be like Jesus Christ.

This is what Romans 8:28–29 says: "We know that in all things God works for the good of those who love him, who have been called according to his purpose. For those God foreknew he also predestined to be conformed to the likeness of his Son, that he might be the firstborn among many brothers." This is what Romans 12:2 is getting at as well.

Sometimes we also get hung up on the idea that God's will must be something unpleasant, difficult, or irrational. Paul corrects that error by giving us three adjectives to describe the nature of God's will.

It is "good," he says. God is the master of the understatement. So if God says his will is good, he means Good with a capital "G." He means that his will for us is the best thing that could possibly be.

God's will is also "pleasing," says Paul. This means acceptable to us, since the fact that God's will is acceptable to God goes without saying. So do not say that the will of God is unpleasant or unacceptable. Or difficult.

Or irrational. If you are thinking along those lines, it is because you have not yet learned to surrender to it. Those who do surrender to God's will, offering their whole selves as sacrifices to him, find that the will of God is the most acceptable thing there can be.

Finally, Paul argues that the will of God is "perfect." No one can say more than that. Human ways are flawed. They can always be improved upon and often must be corrected. God's ways are perfect. They can never be improved upon. So isn't it the most reasonable thing in the world to serve God and to do so without reservation and with all your heart?

4. *It is reasonable because God is worthy of our very best efforts.* We read in Revelation 4:11 the elders' words of praise before God's throne:

> You are worthy, our Lord and God,
>   to receive glory and honor and power,
> for you created all things,
>   and by your will they were created
>   and have their being.

Or again, of Jesus, in Revelation 5:9–10:

> You are worthy to take the scroll
>   and to open its seals,
> because you were slain,
>   and with your blood you purchased men for God
>   from every tribe and language and people and
>   nation.
> You have made them to be a kingdom and priests to
>   serve our God,
>   and they will reign on the earth.

And again:

> Worthy is the Lamb, who was slain,

to receive power and wealth and wisdom and strength
and honor and glory and praise! (v. 12).

That is the testimony of the elders, the four living creatures, the angels, and indeed the entire company of the
redeemed. It affirms that God is worthy of all honor,
including the very best we have to offer.

Do you believe that?

I think therein lies our problem. If we really believed
it, we would judge it reasonable to live for Jesus now, and
we would do it. Instead, in many cases we only *say*, "Jesus
is worthy of all honor," and then we go out and fail to
live for him. Our actions refute our profession.

On the other hand, if you do live for him, giving God
all you can ever hope to be, you are testifying that God
truly is a great God and that he is worthy of the very best
you or anyone else can offer.

5. *It is reasonable because only spiritual things will
last.* My last point is that it is reasonable to give everything we have for God because in the final analysis only
that which is spiritual will endure. Everything else,
everything we see and touch and handle and sometimes
even covet here, will pass away. Jesus said, "Heaven and
earth will pass away" (Matt. 24:35). If that is true of the
entire universe, it is certainly true of the small perishable things that you and I give so much of our lives for.

On the other hand, although "the world and its
desires pass away," we are also told that the one who
"does the will of God lives forever" (1 John 2:17). And
so do that person's works! The Bible says, "Blessed are
the dead who die in the Lord. . . . They will rest from
their labor, [and] their deeds will follow them" (Rev.
14:13). Learning to think this way is part of what it
means to think spiritually. It is a start in developing a
truly Christian mind.

I close with two illustrations. Jim Elliot, that young missionary who died in the jungles of Ecuador, wrote on one occasion, "He is no fool who gives what he cannot keep to gain what he cannot lose." Elliot gave his life to God in what he judged to be the most reasonable service, and he gained a spiritual inheritance forever.

The second example is another missionary whose name was William Borden. He came from a wealthy and privileged family, was a graduate of Yale University, and had the promise of a wonderful and lucrative career before him. But he felt a call to serve God as a missionary in China and left for the field even though his family and friends thought him a fool for going. After a short time away and even before he reached China, Borden contracted a fatal disease and died. He had given up everything to follow Jesus. He died possessing nothing in this world. But "Borden of Yale" did not regret it. We know this because he left a note as he lay dying in Egypt that said, "No reserve, no retreat, and no regrets." Like so many others, he found the service of Christ to be eminently reasonable and gained a lasting reward.

The Pattern of This Age

"Do not conform any longer to *the pattern of this world*"

For secularism, all life, every human value, every human activity must be understood in light of this present time. . . . What matters is now and only now. All access to the above and the beyond is blocked. There is no exit from the confines of this present world.

R. C. Sproul

There are some verses in the Bible that are enriched when we read them in several translations. Romans 12:2 is one of them. In the New International Version the first part of Romans 12:2 says, "Do not conform any longer to the pattern of this world."

This verse has two key words: "world," which is actually "age" (*aiôn*, meaning, "this present age" in contrast to "the age to come"), and "do not conform," which is a compound having at its root the word for "scheme." So the verse means, "Do not let the age in which you live force you into its scheme of thinking and behaving." This is what some of the translations try to bring out. The New American Catholic Bible says, "Do not conform yourselves to this age." The Jerusalem Bible says, "Do not model yourselves on the behavior of the world around you." The Living Bible reads, "Don't copy the behavior and customs of this world." Best known is the paraphrase of J. B. Phillips: "Don't let the world around you squeeze you into its mold."

The idea in each of these renderings is that the world has certain ways of thinking and doing things and is exerting pressure on Christians to conform to those ways. But instead of being conformed, Paul is saying, Christians are to be changed from within to be increasingly like Jesus Christ.

What Is "Worldliness"?

The first phrase of verse 2 is a warning against worldliness. But as soon as we say "worldly" or "worldliness," we have to stop and make very clear what those terms really mean. When I was growing up in a rather fundamentalist church I was taught that worldliness was such "worldly" pursuits as smoking, drinking, dancing, and playing cards. So a Christian girl would say,

> I don't smoke, and I don't chew,
> And I don't go with boys who do.

That is not what Romans 12:2 is about, however. To think of worldliness only in those terms is to trivialize what is a far more serious and far subtler problem.

The clue to what is in view here is that in the next phrase Paul urges, as an alternative to being "conformed" to this world, being "transformed *by the renewing of your mind"* (emphasis mine). This means that he is concerned about a way of thinking rather than mere behaving, though right behavior will follow naturally if our thinking is set straight. In other words, the worldliness we are to break away from and repudiate is the world's "world view," what the Germans call a *Weltanschauung,* a systematic way of looking at all things. We are to break out of the world's categories of thinking and instead let our minds be molded by the Word of God.

Christians in our day have not done this very well, and that is the reason why they are so often "worldly" in the other senses, too. In fact, it is a sad commentary on our time, verified by surveys, that Christians in general have mostly the same thought categories, values, and behavior patterns as the world around them.

Secularism: "The Cosmos Is All That Is"

If worldliness is not such things as smoking, drinking, dancing, and playing cards, what is it? If it is a way of thinking, what is a worldly "world view"? This is something we need to approach in a variety of ways, since there is no single word that is perfectly descriptive of how the world thinks. On the other hand, if there is a word that most accurately describes the world's way of thinking, it is *secularism.* Secularism is an umbrella term that covers a number of other "isms," like humanism, relativism, pragmatism, pluralism, hedonism, and materialism. But more than any other single word, it

aptly describes the mental framework and value struc-
ture of the people of our time.

The word *secular* also comes closest to what Paul actually says when he refers to "the pattern of this world."
The word is derived from the Latin word *saeculum,*
which means "age." And the word found in Paul's phrase
in verse 2 is the exact Greek equivalent. Our version uses
the noun "world," but the Greek actually says, "Do not
be conformed to this *age.*" In other words, "Do not be
'secularist' in your world view."

There is a right way to be secular, of course. Christians
live in the world and are therefore rightly concerned
about the world's affairs. We have legitimate secular concerns. But secularism (note the "ism") is more than this.
It is a philosophy that does not look beyond this world
but instead operates as if this age is all there is.

The best single statement of secularism I know is
something Carl Sagan said in the television series "Cosmos." He was pictured standing before a spectacular
view of the starry night heaven with its many swirling
galaxies, saying in a hushed, almost reverential tone of
voice, "The cosmos is all that is or ever was or ever will
be." That is secularism "in your face." It is bound up
entirely by the limits of the material universe, by what
we can see and touch and weigh and measure. If we think
in terms of our existence here, secularism means operating within the limits of life on earth. If we are thinking of time, it means disregarding the eternal and thinking only of the "now."

This is expressed in popular advertising slogans like
"You only go around once" and Pepsi's "Now Generation." These slogans dominate our culture and express
an outlook that has become increasingly harmful. If
"now" is the only thing that matters, why should we
worry about the national debt, for example? That's not
our problem. Let our children worry about it. Or why

should we study hard and prepare to do meaningful work later on in life instead of having a good time now? Most important, why should we worry about God or righteousness or sin or judgment or salvation, if there is no beyond and "now" is all that matters?

R. C. Sproul writes, "For secularism, all life, every human value, every human activity must be understood in light of this present time.... What matters is *now* and only *now*. All access to the above and the beyond is *blocked*. There is no exit from the confines of this present world. The secular is all that we have. We must make our decisions, live our lives, make our plans, all within the closed arena of this time—the here and now."[1]

Each of us should recognize that description instantly, because it is the viewpoint we are surrounded with every single day of our lives and in every conceivable place and circumstance.

Yet that is the outlook we must refuse to accept. Instead of being conformed to this world, as if that is all there is, we are to see all things as relating to God and to eternity. Here is the contrast, as expressed by Harry Blamires: "To think secularly is to think within a frame of reference bounded by the limits of our life on earth; it is to keep one's calculations rooted in this-worldly criteria. To think Christianly is to accept all things with the mind as related, directly or indirectly, to man's eternal destiny as the redeemed and chosen child of God."[2]

Humanism: "You Will Be Like God"

We have seen that there is a proper concern for secular things that even Christians should have, though secularism as a world view is wrong. The same qualification holds for this next popular "ism," *humanism*.

Obviously, there is a proper kind of humanism, meaning a view that reflects a proper concern for human beings. "Humanitarianism" is a better word for that. People who care for other people are humanitarians. But there is also a philosophical humanism, which is a way of looking at people, particularly ourselves, apart from God, and this is not at all right. Rather, it is both wrong and very harmful. Instead of looking at people biblically, this is a secular way of looking at them, which is why we so often couple the adjective to the noun and speak more fully, not just of humanism but of "secular humanism" instead.

The best example of secular humanism I know is in the Book of Daniel. One day Nebuchadnezzar, the great king of Babylon, was on the roof of his palace, looking out over his splendid hanging gardens to the prosperous city beyond. He was impressed with his handiwork and said, "Is not this the great Babylon I have built as the royal residence, by my mighty power and for the glory of my majesty?" (Dan. 4:30). This was secular humanism—a statement that everything he saw was "of" him, "by" him, and "for" the glory of his own majesty. This kind of humanism says that everything revolves around man and exists for man's glory.

God would not tolerate such arrogance. So he judged Nebuchadnezzar with insanity, indicating that this is a crazy philosophy. Nebuchadnezzar was then driven out to live with the beasts, and he acted like a beast until at last he acknowledged that God alone is the true ruler of the universe and that everything exists for God's glory rather than ours:

> I, Nebuchadnezzar, raised my eyes toward heaven, and my sanity was restored. Then I praised the Most High; I honored and glorified him who lives forever.
>
> His dominion is an eternal dominion. . . .

> He does as he pleases
>> with the powers of heaven
>> and the peoples of the earth.

Daniel 4:34–35

Humanism is opposed to God and hostile to Christianity. This has always been so, but it is especially evident in the public statements of modern humanism: *A Humanist Manifesto* (1933), *Humanist Manifesto II* (1973), and *The Secularist Humanist Declaration* (1980). The first of these, the 1933 document, said, "Traditional theism, especially faith in the prayer-hearing God, assumed to love and care for persons, to hear and understand their prayers, and to be able to do something about them, is an unproved and outmoded faith. Salvationism, based on mere affirmation, still appears as harmful, diverting people with false hopes of heaven hereafter. Reasonable minds look to other means for survival."[3]

The 1973 *Humanist Manifesto II* said, "We find insufficient evidence for belief in the existence of a supernatural"[4] and "There is no credible evidence that life survives the death of the body."[5]

Where does humanism lead, then? It leads to a deification of self and, contrary to what it professes, to a growing disregard for other people.

In deifying self, humanism actually deifies nearly everything but God. Several years ago, Herbert Schlossberg, one of the project directors for the Fieldstead Institute, wrote a book titled *Idols for Destruction* in which he showed how humanism has made gods of history, mammon, nature, power, religion, and, of course, humanity itself.[6] It is brilliantly done.

As for disregarding other people, well, look at the bestsellers of the 1970s. You will find titles like *Winning Through Intimidation* and *Looking Out for Number One*.

These books say, in a manner utterly consistent with secular humanism, "Forget about other people; look out for yourself; you are what matters." What emerged in those years is what Tom Wolfe, the social critic, called the "Me Decade." And the 1970s gave way to the 1980s, which others have aptly called "the golden age of greed."

Remember, too, that this is the philosophy (some would say religion) underlying public-school education. This is ironic, of course, since humanism is an irrational philosophy. It is irrational because it is impossible to establish humanistic or any other values or goals without a transcendent point of reference, and it is precisely that transcendent point that is being repudiated by the humanists. Frighteningly, the irrationalism of humanism is appearing in the chaos of the schools, where students are using guns and knives to kill their classmates and threaten teachers whom they hold in contempt.

In 1992 an ABC "PrimeTime Live" television special, featuring Diane Sawyer, reported that in this country one in five students comes to school with a handgun somewhat regularly, and that there are ten times as many knives in schools as there are guns. What is more, this is as true of the suburbs as it is of the inner city. In Wichita, Kansas, which calls itself mid-America, students must now pass through metal detectors before entering school, and there are still guns and other weapons found in the buildings. Scores of other school districts are installing such detectors and other security measures to stem the increasing tide of violence.

For humanism as well as for secularism, the word for Christians is "do not conform any longer." And remember that the first expression of humanism was not the *Humanist Manifesto* of 1933 or even the arrogant words of Nebuchadnezzar spoken about six hundred years before Christ, but the words of Satan in the Garden of

Eden, when he told Eve, "You will be like God, knowing good and evil" (Gen. 3:5).

Relativism: "A Moral Morass"

We also need to think briefly about *relativism,* because,
if man is the focal point of everything, there are no
absolutes in any area of life and everything is up for
grabs. Some years ago, Professor Allan Bloom of the University of Chicago wrote a book called *The Closing of the
American Mind,* in which he said on the very first page,
"There is one thing a professor can be absolutely certain
of: almost every student entering the university believes,
or says he believes, that truth is relative."[7]
What that book set out to prove is that education is
impossible in such a climate. People can learn skills in
school, of course. You can be trained to drive a truck,
work a computer, handle financial transactions, and do
scores of other things. But real education, which means
learning to sift through error to discover what is true,
good, and beautiful, is impossible, because the goals of
real education—truth, goodness, and beauty—do not
exist for the relativist. And even if they did exist in some
far-off metaphysical never-never land, it would be
impossible to find them, because it requires absolutes
even to discover absolutes. It requires such absolutes as
the laws of logic, for example.
Is it any wonder that with such an underlying destructive philosophy as relativism, not to mention secularism
and humanism, America is experiencing what *Time* magazine called "a moral morass" and "a values vacuum."[8]

Materialism: "The Material Girl"

The final "ism" I want to discuss as representative of
"the pattern of this world" to which Christians are not

to be conformed is *materialism*. This takes us back to
secularism, of which it is both a part and a side effect. If
"the cosmos is all there is or ever was or ever will be,"
it follows that nothing exists but what is material or mea-
surable, and if there is any value to be found in life, it
must be in material terms. Be as healthy as you can. Live
as long as you can. Get as rich as you can.

Who are the heroes of our day? When today's young
people are asked whom they admire and want to emu-
late, what comes out rather quickly is that they have
no people they actually look up to except possibly the
rich and the famous in the entertainment world—
people like Michael Jackson and Madonna. And speaking of Madonna, isn't it interesting that she is referred
to most often not as a singer or entertainer or even a sex
symbol but as "the material girl." That is, she repre-
sents the material things of this world, clothes (or the
lack of them), money, fame, and above all pleasure. And
this is what today's young people want to be like! They
want to be rich and famous and own things and enjoy
them. They want to be like Madonna.

The poet T. S. Eliot wrote an epitaph for our materialistic generation:

> Here were a decent godless people:
> Their only monument the asphalt road
> And a thousand lost golf balls.

How different a hero is the Lord Jesus Christ! He was
born into a poor family, was laid in a borrowed manger
for a cradle at his birth, never had a home or a bank
account or a family of his own.

He said of himself, "Foxes have holes and birds of the
air have nests, but the Son of Man has no place to lay his
head" (Matt. 8:20).

At his trial before Pilate he said, "My kingdom is not of this world. If it were, my servants would fight. . . . My kingdom is from another place" (John 18:36).

When he died he was laid in a borrowed tomb.

If there was ever an individual who operated on the basis of values above and beyond the world in which we live, it was Jesus Christ. He was the polar opposite of "the material girl." But at the same time no one has ever affected this world for good as much as the Lord Jesus Christ has. And it is into his image that we are to be "transformed" rather than being forced into the mold of this world's sinful and destructive "isms."

No One But Jesus

In the next few studies we are going to explore another aspect of the problem presented by today's world and begin to look at the solution proposed by Paul in Romans 12:2. But I want to close this study by looking ahead one phrase to what Paul says we are to be: not "conformed" but *"transformed"* by the renewing of our minds. There is a deliberate distinction between those two words, as I am sure you can see. Conformity is something that happens to you outwardly. Transformation happens inwardly. You will see this at once when I tell you that the Greek word translated "transformed" is *metamorphoô,* from which we get "metamorphosis." It is what happens to the lowly caterpillar when it turns into a beautiful butterfly.

And there is another interesting fact. This Greek word is found four times in the New Testament: once here, once in 2 Corinthians 3:18 to describe our being transformed into the glorious likeness of Jesus Christ, and twice in the Gospels, in reference to the transfiguration of Jesus on the mountain where he had gone with Peter, James, and John. Those verses say, "There he was transfigured before them" (Matt. 17:2; Mark 9:2). It is the same word. That is, the same word used by Paul to describe our transformation by the renewing of our minds, so that we will not be conformed to this world, is used by the Gospel writers to describe the transfiguration of Jesus from the form of his earthly humiliation to the radiance that Peter, James, and John were privileged to witness for a time.

And that is why Paul writes as he does in 2 Corinthians, saying, "We, who with unveiled faces all reflect the Lord's glory, are being transformed into his likeness with ever-increasing glory, which comes from the Lord, who is the Spirit" (3:18).

In 2 Corinthians Paul says, "It is happening," but in Romans 12 he says, "Let it happen," thus putting upon us the responsibility, though not the power, to accomplish this necessary transformation. How does it happen? It happens through the renewing of our minds, and the way our minds become renewed is by studying the life-giving and renewing Word of God. Without that study, we will remain in the world's mold, unable to think correctly and therefore also unable to act as Christians. With that study, blessed and empowered as it will be by the Holy Spirit, we will begin to take on something of the glorious luster of the Lord Jesus Christ and become increasingly like him.

This Mindless Age

"the pattern of this world"

Has God created us rational beings, and shall we deny our humanity which he has given us? Has God spoken to us, and shall we not listen to his words? Has God renewed our mind through Christ, and shall we not think with it?

John R. W. Stott

When we think of the cultural patterns that dominate the world we live in, we think first and naturally of the philosophies or "isms" we looked at in the previous study—secularism, humanism, relativism, and materialism, which is why I began with them. But there is another cultural pattern that may be even more significant for most of us than those philosophies. It is what I call "mindlessness," that is, the inability or at least the unwillingness to look at what is happening around us in an analytical and critical way.

Since Christians are called to mind renewal—Romans 12:2 says, "Do not conform any longer to the pattern of this world, but be transformed by the renewing of your mind"—this cultural mindlessness must be an aspect of "the pattern of this world" that we are to recognize, understand, and overcome. We are to be many things as Christians, but one requirement that is certainly high on the list, if not foundational to everything, is to be thinking people.

America Has Been "Vannatized"

There are a number of causes for our present mindlessness—western materialism, the fast pace of modern life, and philosophical skepticism, among others. We will not think deeply if all we are concerned about is earning money. We will not think deeply if we are rushing around madly all the time and are therefore too busy to think. We will not think deeply if we do not believe thinking is worthwhile. These are some important factors contributing to our present mindless climate. But I want to argue here that the chief cause of our mindlessness is television.

I began to study television as a cultural problem several years ago after I had read a 1987 graduation address at Duke University by Ted Koppel of ABC's "Nightline" news program. Following this address, Koppel was frequently quoted by Christian communicators because of something he said about the Ten Commandments, which is why I sent away for his remarks in the first place. He was deploring the declining moral tone of our country and reminded his predominantly secular audience of the abiding validity of this religious standard. He said that they are Ten Commandments, not "ten suggestions," and that they "are," not "were" the standard.

But to me the most interesting thing about Koppel's address was not what he said about the Ten Commandments, however true it was, but what he said in the very first sentence of his remarks. He said, "America has been 'Vannatized.'"

Vannatized? What's that?

Koppel was referring to Vanna White, the beautiful and extraordinarily popular young lady on the television game show "Wheel of Fortune." For years now, Vanna White has been something of a phenomenon on television. As far as her work goes, it is simple. She stands on one side of a large game board that holds blocks representing the letters of words the contestants are supposed to guess. As they guess correctly, Vanna walks across the stage, turning the blocks around to reveal the letters. When she gets to the other side she claps her hands. It is simple work, but Vanna seems to like it.

No, "like" is too mild a term, as Koppel notes. Vanna "thrills, rejoices, adores everything she sees." People respond to her so well that books about her have appeared in bookstores, and she is well up on that magical but elusive list of the most-admired people in America.

But here is the interesting thing. Until recently, Vanna never said a word on "Wheel of Fortune," and Koppel asked how a person who says nothing and who is therefore basically unknown to us can be so popular. That is just the point, he answered. Since we do not know what Vanna White is actually like, she is whatever we want her to be. "Is she a feminist or every male chauvinist's dream? She is whatever you want her to be. Sister, lover, daughter, friend, never cross, non-threatening and non-judgmental to a fault."[1] She is popular because we can project our own deep feelings, needs, or fantasies onto her television image.

Koppel does not care very much about the success of "Wheel of Fortune," of course. He was analyzing our culture. And his point is that Vanna White's appeal is the very essence of television and that television forms our way of thinking or, to be more accurate, of *not* thinking. It has been hailed as a great teaching tool, but teaching is precisely what it does not do, because it seldom presents anything in enough depth for a person actually to think about it. Instead, it presents thirty-second flashes of events and offers images upon which we are invited to project our own vague feelings.

If all we are talking about is game shows and other forms of television entertainment, none of this would matter very much, except for the amount of time our children spend watching these banal, mind-numbing diversions rather than disciplining their minds by serious study. But if television is really conditioning us not to think, as Koppel and I maintain, then television poses a serious intellectual, social, and spiritual problem.

Amusing Ourselves to Death

A more academic study of the negative impact of television on culture has been provided by Neil Postman, a professor of communication arts and sciences at New York University. It is called *Amusing Ourselves to Death: Public Discourse in the Age of Show Business.*[2]

Amusing Ourselves to Death was first published one year after 1984, the year popularized as the title of George Orwell's futuristic novel, with its dark vision of a society controlled by fear. In Orwell's novel, Big Brother rules everything with a ruthless iron fist. But Postman reminds us that there was another novel written slightly earlier that had an equally chilling but quite different vision of the future: *Brave New World* by Aldous Huxley. In Huxley's novel, there is no need for Big Brother because, in this ominous vision of the future, people have come to love both their oppression and the technologies that strip away their capacities to think.

Writes Postman:

> What Orwell feared were those who would ban books. What Huxley feared was that there would be no reason to ban a book, for there would be no one who wanted to read one. Orwell feared those who would deprive us of information. Huxley feared those who would give us so much that we would be reduced to passivity and egoism. Orwell feared that the truth would be concealed from us. Huxley feared the truth would be drowned in a sea of irrelevance. Orwell feared we would become a captive culture. Huxley feared we would become a trivial culture. . . . As Huxley remarked in *Brave New World Revisited*, the civil libertarians and rationalists who are ever on the alert to oppose tyranny "failed to take into account man's almost infinite appetite for diversions."[3]

Obviously, the western cultures, led by the United States of America, have succumbed to the second of these two oppressions, just as the communist countries fell victim to the first.

So what does Postman say? The first half of his book is a study of the difference between what he calls "the age of typography" and our present television age, which he calls "the age of show business." Typography refers to words in print, and it concerns the communication of ideas by newspapers, pamphlets, and books. It is rational and analytic, because that is the way written words work.

When we read something that requires us to think, there is a certain distance between ourselves and the printed page. We read, but we are not necessarily swept along with what we read. We analyze, ponder, weigh, compare, contrast, and disagree. We re-read a paragraph if we do not understand the argument. If we are pursuing a technical paper, we may look up vocabulary we do not know. We follow the arguments, and we disagree with them if they seem to be inadequate. We may challenge the conclusions. There is even a certain distance between ourselves and more popular writing, which is why we do not cheer a well-written sentence or applaud a powerful paragraph, though we may appreciate how well the work is done. People who read well and are conditioned by the written word can and do think. Written words promote thinking. Moreover, the more skillfully people read and the more they read, the better and longer they can think.

Postman illustrates the strength of typography by the public attention given to the famous Lincoln/Douglas debates of the mid-1800s, which people were capable of hearing (or reading), understanding, and forming opinions about, even though they lasted three to seven hours. Their minds had been developed by the printed page. Unfortunately, television does not operate by rational means of communication but by images, as Ted Koppel pointed out. As a result we are becoming an unthinking culture.

A great deal of what Postman develops in his book is reinforcement for what I have been describing as mindlessness. So let me review three specific areas of bad influence, as he sees it.

News on Television: "Now . . . This"

There is a chapter in Postman's book that deals with news on television, and it is entitled "Now . . . This." Those are the words most used on television to link one brief televised news segment—the average news segment on network news programs is only forty-five seconds long—to the next news segment or a commercial. What the phrase means is that what one has just seen has no relevance to what one is about to see next or, for that matter, to anything. Rational thought requires such connections. Thinking depends on similarities, contradictions, deductions, and the development of probable consequences. That requires time. It is what books and other print media can give us, as I said. But this is precisely what most television does not give, because it does not allow time for thought. And if it does not provide time for thought or promote thought, what it essentially amounts to is "diversion."

Postman says that television gives us "news without consequences, without value, and therefore without essential seriousness; that is to say, news as pure entertainment."[4] In other words, it is not only mindless; it is teaching us to be mindless, to the point at which we even suppose that our ignorance is great knowledge.

Politics: "Reach Out and Elect Someone"

A second area of bad influence in our television age is politics. Postman calls this chapter "Reach Out and Elect Someone." Ronald Reagan once said, "Politics is just like show business."[5] But if this is so, then the object of politics on television is not to pursue excellence, clarity, or honesty, or any other generally recognized virtue, but to make it appear as if you are doing so.

After the 1968 presidential campaign, in which Richard Nixon finally won the White House, a political writer named Joe McGinniss wrote a book titled *The Selling of the President 1968*. In it he described the strategy of the Nixon advisors, who felt that their candidate had lost the 1960 election to John F. Kennedy because of Kennedy's better television image. He reports that William Gavin, one of Nixon's chief aides, advised, "Break away from linear logic: present a barrage of impressions, of attitudes. Break off in mid-sentence and skip to something half a world away. . . . Reason pushes the viewer back, it assaults him, it demands that he agree or disagree; impression can envelop him, invite him in, without making an intellectual demand. . . . Get the voters to like the guy, and the battle's two-thirds won."[6]

How do campaign managers get their candidates elected these days? It is not by discussing issues. That is a sure way to get defeated, because any position on any issue, unless it is utterly meaningless, is certain to offend somebody. The way to win elections is to present a pleasant television image and keep the candidate out of trouble for as long as possible.

That is why Ronald Reagan won the presidency in 1980 and won even more decisively in 1984. It was not his positions, though they were substantially different from those of his predecessors and opponents and were, in my opinion, generally correct. There really was "a Reagan revolution," but this was not why he won. He won mainly because he had a long career in movies and was a master of the television medium. He projected the image of a strong and decent man we could trust.

In the next election, the election of 1988, George Bush defeated Michael Dukakis. That was an election involving some genuine issues about which every intelligent voter should have been informed. Television is supposed to be the medium through which this can be done. But a discussion of the issues is precisely what the voters did not get. Where did George Bush and Michael Dukakis differ in their politics? In regard to domestic issues such as Social Security, child care, education, taxes, and abortion? In international affairs? The military? Relations with Russia, Eastern Europe, China, Japan? It is only specialists in government who have any idea what the true answers to those questions are, not the voters, because these were not the issues of the campaign.

What were the issues, then? Actually, there was only one real issue, and it was this: Is George Bush a "wimp"?

Why was that raised? It was because Bush looked like a wimp on television: he is thin, seems to be frail, and often held his head slightly to one side in a way that looked deferential. If the Dukakis camp could encourage voters to think of Bush that way, they would vote for Dukakis, because no one wants a weakling for president. On the other hand, Bush's task was to convince the voters that he would actually be a strong president, and the strategy of his camp was therefore to wage a strong, aggressive campaign against Dukakis that many said was "unfair" and "nasty."

The media complained! Dan Rather, Tom Brokaw, and Peter Jennings were predictably self-righteous and offended. They called it the least substantial, meanest campaign in memory. But how hypocritical! Yes, it was mindless politics, but it was mindless precisely because that is what television demands. It promotes images, not thought.

And what about the campaign of 1992? I had said from the beginning that Bill Clinton would win the election, not because he had a better program for getting the country out of debt or even because the electorate was unhappy with America's slow economic growth in the previous few years, but because Clinton looked better on television. He was the perfect television candidate, and so he won.

Marshall McLuhan was right when he said, "The medium *is* the message." Campaign managers have learned that lesson well, which is why they organize the kinds of campaigns they do.

A person may protest that Ronald Reagan *was* a decent, strong man, or say that "George Bush really *was* a wimp [or was *not* a wimp]," or that Bill Clinton *was* the better candidate. But my point is that we do not actually know those things and cannot know them, at least from television, until future events either support or fail to support our perceptions. Perhaps the most serious thing of all is not that we do not know, but that we think we *do* know, because of television.

Religion as Entertainment

The third area where television has a bad influence is religion, which is where Postman's study gets particularly close to our concerns here. His chapter on religion is called "Shuffle Off to Bethlehem."

Religion is chiefly presented on television in an entertainment format. With the possible exception of Billy Graham, who has a national and even international following quite apart from television, and some other teaching pastors such as Charles Stanley and D. James Kennedy, the stars of religious television are mostly entertainers. Pat Robertson is a master of ceremonies along the lines of Merv Griffin. Jimmy Swaggart, who was an extremely successful religious television figure before his fall through immorality, is a piano player and singer as well as having been a vivacious and entertaining speaker. Even televised church services, like those of Jerry Falwell and Robert Schuller, contain their requisite musical numbers and pop testimonies, just like the variety shows on secular television. The proper name for that is vaudeville.

But here is the important question: What is lost in the translation of religion to television? The answer is: Nearly everything that makes religion real. The chief loss is a sense of the transcendent. God is missing. Postman says, "Everything that makes religion an historic, profound and sacred human activity is stripped away; there is no ritual, no dogma, no tradition, no theology, and above all, no sense of spiritual transcendence. On these shows, the preacher is tops. God comes out as second banana."[7]

In another place he says, "If I am not mistaken, the word for this is blasphemy."[8]

An observer who likes such religious entertainment might object, "Well, what harm is done as long as genuine religion is still to be found in church on Sundays?" But is it? I would argue that so pervasive and normalizing is the impact of television that pressures have inevitably come to make church services as irrelevant and entertaining as the tube.

In the vast majority of church services today, there are virtually no pastoral prayers, much brainless music, chummy chatter, and abbreviated sermons. And what are preachers told? They are told to be personable, to relate funny stories, to smile, above all to stay away from topics that might cause people to become unhappy with the church and leave it. One extremely popular television preacher will not talk about sin, on the grounds that doing so makes people feel bad. Preachers are to preach to felt needs, not necessarily real needs, and this generally means telling people only what they want to hear.

Was Jesus amusing? Were Martin Luther, John Calvin, John Wesley, or Jonathan Edwards entertainers?

Your Mind Matters

This is the point at which we need to talk about genuine mind renewal for Christians, which is what I will continue with in the next chapter. But I close here by mentioning a helpful little book by John Stott, the Rector Emeritus of All Souls Church in London. It is titled *Your Mind Matters.* The book deals with six spheres of Christian living, and it argues that each one is impossible without a proper and energetic use of our minds: Christian worship, Christian faith, Christian holiness, Christian guidance, Christian evangelism, and Christian ministry.

We must use our minds in *worship,* because worship is honoring God for who he is, and in order to do that we must understand something about his attributes. In other words, we must praise him for being sovereign, holy, merciful, wise, and so on.

We must use our minds in areas requiring *faith,* because faith is believing the word or promises of God, and to believe God's word or promises we must understand what they are.

We must use our minds in our growth in *holiness,* because sanctification is not a matter of emotional experience or simply following out a formula for sanctification—the two most popular approaches to sanctification today—but, rather, knowing what God has done in us when he joined us to Christ, and then acting upon it. It is knowing that we cannot go back to being what we were and therefore that there is no direction for us to go but forward.

We must use our minds in seeking personal *guidance* as to how we should live and what decisions we must make, because the principles by which we must be guided are in the Bible. We need to study them, understand them, and apply them. This cannot be done without thinking.

We must use our minds in *evangelism,* because if faith is necessary for a person to be saved and if faith is responding to the Word of God and acting on it (as I have just written), we are obliged to present the teachings of the Bible and the claims of Jesus Christ so people can understand them. If they do not understand what they are called upon to "believe" and therefore only respond emotionally, their "faith" is not true faith and theirs is not a true conversion. They will drop away eventually, as many supposed "converts" do.

We must use our minds in *ministry,* first, in seeking out a sphere of service ("What am I good at? Where do

my spiritual gifts lie? What is God leading me to do for
him?") and, second, to serve in that sphere of work well
("How should I go about the work I have been given?").

Stott argues that "anti-intellectualism . . . is . . . part
of the fashion of the world and therefore a form of worldliness. To denigrate the mind is to undermine foundational Christian doctrines." He asks pointedly, "Has God
created us rational beings, and shall we deny our humanity which he has given us? Has God spoken to us,
and shall we not listen to his words? Has God renewed
our mind through Christ, and shall we not think with it?
Is God going to judge us by his Word, and shall we not
be wise and build our house upon this rock?"[9]

They are important and helpful questions, if you *think*
about them.

Thinking Christianly

"but be *transformed* by the renewing of your mind"

There is nothing in our experience, however trivial, worldly, or even evil, which cannot be thought about Christianly. There is likewise nothing in our experience, however sacred, which cannot be thought about secularly. . . .

Harry Blamires

I have several times mentioned the name of Harry Blamires, an Englishman who has written two good works on what it means to have a Christian mind: *The Christian Mind: How Should a Christian Think?* (1963) and *Recovering the Christian Mind: Meeting the Challenge of Secularism* (1988). In each of these volumes

Blamires encourages us to reject the world's thinking and begin to think as Christians, which is what the apostle Paul is writing about in our text from Romans 12: "Do not conform any longer to the pattern of this world, but be transformed by the renewing of your mind . . ." (v. 2). This means that our thinking is not to be determined by the culture of the world around us, but instead we are to have a distinctly different and growing Christian world view and life view.

But what does it actually mean to have such an outlook? Or, to put it in slightly different terms: How are we to experience mind renewal in our exceedingly mindless age?

Thinking Christianly and Thinking Secularly

The one thing this mind renewal does not mean is what most people probably assume it does mean, and that is to start thinking mainly about Christian subjects. We do need to think about Christian subjects, of course. In fact, it is from that base of revealed doctrine and its applications to life that we can begin to "think Christianly" about other matters. I am going to pursue exactly that line of thought in this study. However, thinking Christianly is not a matter of thinking about Christian subjects as opposed to thinking about secular subjects, as many people suppose, but rather thinking in a Christian way about everything—having a Christian mind.

This is because, by contrast, it is possible to think in a secular way even about religious subjects. Take the Lord's Supper, for instance. For most Christians the Lord's Supper is probably the most spiritual of all religious worship experiences. Yet it is possible to think about even the Lord's Supper in a worldly manner. Perhaps someone who is a trustee of the church might be thinking that he forgot to include the cost of the communion elements in the next year's budget. Another communicant might be looking at the minister and criticizing his way of handling the elements. "He's so awkward," this person might be thinking. Still another person might be reflecting on how good it is for people to have spiritual thoughts or to observe religious ceremonies, but in the same framework by which he might also conclude that it is good for tense executives to play golf or harried housewives to spend a few afternoons by themselves shopping. Each of these persons would be thinking in a secular way about the most sacred of Christian practices.

On the other hand, it is possible to think Christianly about even the most mundane matters. Blamires suggests how we might do this at a gasoline station while we are waiting for our tank to be filled. We might be reflecting on how a mechanized world with cars and other machines tends to make God seem unnecessary, or how a speeded-up world in which we use planes or cars to race from one appointment to another makes it difficult to think deeply about people or even care for them. Even further, we might be wondering, Do material things like cars really serve us, or are we enslaved to them? Do they cause us to covet and therefore break the Tenth Commandment? And what about engine exhausts and other pollutants? Don't they threaten the environment over which God has made us stewards? And if they do, what can be done about it?

Blamires says, "There is nothing in our experience, however trivial, worldly, or even evil, which cannot be thought about Christianly. There is likewise nothing in our experience, however sacred, which cannot be thought about secularly—considered, that is to say, simply in its relationship to the passing existence of bodies and psyches in a time-locked universe."[1]

The God Who Is There

So where do we start? How do we begin to think and act as Christians? There is a sense in which we could begin at any point, since truth is a whole and truth in any one area will inevitably lead to truth in every other area. But if the dominant philosophy of our day is secularism—which means viewing all of life only in terms of the visible world and in terms of the here and now—then the best of all possible starting places is the doctrine of God, for God alone is above and beyond the world and is eternal. Even more, the doctrine of God is a necessary and inevitable starting place if we are to produce a genuinely Christian response to secularism.

What does that mean for our thinking?

Well, if there is a God, this very fact means that the supernatural is a reality. The word *supernatural* means "over," "above," or "in addition to nature." In other words, to go back to Carl Sagan, who says, "The cosmos is all there is or ever was or ever will be," Christians say the cosmos is *not* all there is or was or ever will be. God is. God exists. He is there, whether we acknowledge this truth or not, and he stands behind the cosmos. He was before the cosmos. In fact, it is only *because* there is a God that there is a cosmos, since without God nothing else could possibly have come to be.

If anything exists, there must be an inevitable, self-existent, uncaused First Cause that stands behind it.

On one occasion Professor John H. Gerstner referred to something his high-school physics teacher had said many years before. The teacher said, "The most profound question that has ever been asked by anybody is: Why is there something rather than nothing?"

Gerstner remarked that he was impressed with that at the time. But later, as he sharpened his ability to think, he recognized that it was not a profound question at all.

In fact, it was not even a true question. It posed an alternative: something rather than nothing. "But what is nothing?" Gerstner asked. "Nothing" eludes definition. It even defies conception. For as soon as you say, "Nothing is . . ." nothing ceases to be nothing and becomes something.

Jonathan Edwards is not known for being funny, but on one occasion he was being at least slightly humorous when he said, "Nothing is what the sleeping rocks dream of." So, commented Gerstner, "Anyone who thinks he knows what nothing is must have those rocks in his head."[2]

As soon as you ask, "Why is there something rather than nothing?" the alternative vanishes, you are left with something, and the only possible explanation for that something is "In the beginning God created the heavens and the earth" (Gen. 1:1), which is what Christianity teaches.

"He Is There and He Is Not Silent"

Before we explore the implications of God's existence for our thinking, I have to introduce another doctrine alongside the doctrine of God, and that is the doctrine of revelation. The God who exists has revealed himself. Francis Schaeffer put this doctrine in the title of one of his books: *He Is There and He Is Not Silent*.[3] That is exactly the point. God is there, and he has not kept himself hidden from us. He has revealed himself—in nature, in history, and especially in the Scriptures.

In chapter 6 I discussed "the pattern of this age" as characterized by secularism, humanism, relativism, and materialism. The doctrine of God is the specific Christian answer to secularism (as well as to everything else, in various senses). Revelation is the specific answer to relativism. If God has spoken, what he has said is truthful and can be trusted absolutely, since God never lies. This gives us absolutes in the universe and a valid sense of security and purpose. People who deny that absolutes exist must inevitably regard the universe as meaningless and chaotic.

That God has spoken and that his word to us can be trusted has always been the conviction of the church, at least until relatively modern times. Today, the truthfulness of the Bible has been challenged but with disastrous results. For, without a sure word from God, all words are equally valid, and Christianity is neither more certain nor more compelling than any other merely human word or philosophy.

But now notice this: If God has spoken, there will always be a certain hardness about the Christian faith and Christians. I do not mean that we will be hard on others or insensitive to them, but that there will be a certain unyielding quality to our convictions. For one thing, we will insist upon truth and will not bow to the notion, however strongly it is pressed upon us, that "that's just your opinion."

Several years ago I was flying to Chicago from the West Coast and got into a conversation with the woman seated next to me. We talked about religion. Whenever I made a statement about the gospel she replied, "But that's just your opinion." She was speaking out of a relativistic mold.

I hit on a way of answering her that preserved the hardness of what I was trying to say and yet did it nicely. I said, "You're right. That is my opinion, but that's not really what matters. What matters is: Is it true?"

She did not know quite what to say to that. So the conversation went on, and after a while she replied to something else I was saying in the same way: "But that's just your opinion."

Again I said, "You're right. That is my opinion, but that's not really what matters. What matters is: Is it true?" This happened about a dozen times, and eventually she began to smile and then laugh as she anticipated my response to her comment. When I got home I sent her a copy of C. S. Lewis's book *Mere Christianity.*

Another thing the doctrine of revelation will mean for us is that we will not back down or compromise on moral issues. You know how it is whenever you speak out against some particularly evil act. If people do not merely say, "But that's just your opinion," they are likely to attack you personally, making accusations like, "You'd do the same thing if you were in her situation" or "Do you think you're better than he is?"

We must not be put off by such attacks. Our response should be something like this: "Please, I wasn't talking about what I would do if I were in that person's shoes. I'm a sinner, too. I might have acted much worse. I would probably have failed sooner. I wasn't talking about that. I was talking about what is right, and I think that is what we need to talk about. None of us is ever going to do better than we are doing unless we talk about it and decide what's right to do."

Cheating—because everybody else does it?

Promiscuity—because that is the modern way of life and "it is nobody's business but our own"?

Abortion—because the law allows it?

Divorce—because it seems the better option to marital discord?

Blamires writes: "What the secular mind is ill-equipped to grasp is that the Christian faith leaves Christians with no choice at all on many matters of this kind."[4] We are people under God's authority, and that authority is expressed for us in the Bible.

The West's Spiritual Exhaustion

Now we are ready to explore some specific implications of the doctrine of God. First, if there is a God and if he has created us to have eternal fellowship with him, then we are going to look at failure, suffering, pain, and even death differently than secularists do. For the Christian, these can never be the greatest of all tragedies. Yes, they are bad. Death is an enemy. First Corinthians 15:26 calls it "the last enemy." But these bad things are over-balanced by eternal realities. Christians can face death calmly, knowing that beyond death they will be with Jesus.

Second, success and pleasure will not be the greatest of all treasures for us. They are good things, but they will never compare with salvation from sin and knowing God. Jesus said it clearly: "What good will it be for a man if he gains the whole world, yet forfeits his soul?" (Matt. 16:26). Or, from the other side, "Do not be afraid of those who kill the body but who cannot kill the soul. Rather, be afraid of the One who can destroy both soul and body in hell" (Matt. 10:28).

And that leads to a Christian response to materialism, another of the "isms" I discussed earlier. There are two kinds of materialism: a philosophical materialism, like that of doctrinaire communism, and a practical materialism, which is most characteristic of the West. We have been raised with a false kind of syllogism that says, "Because we are not communists and communists are materialists, therefore we are not materialists." But that conclusion does not necessarily follow. Most of us embrace a practical materialism that warps our souls, stunts our spiritual growth, and hinders the advance of the gospel in our generation.

The best critique of Western materialism that I know is from Aleksandr Solzhenitsyn, a former citizen of the Soviet Union, now exiled. It is in the form of an address he gave to the graduating class of Harvard University in 1978. Up to this point, Solzhenitsyn was somewhat of an American hero. He had suffered in the Soviet Union's infamous gulag prison system and had later defected, which is why he was invited to speak at Harvard. But in this address he was so blunt in his criticism of the West that his popularity vanished almost overnight, and today he is almost never heard from, though he continues to write voluminously from a retreat in New England.

Solzhenitsyn's address was no defense of socialism. Quite the contrary. He celebrated its ideological defeat in Eastern Europe, saying, "It is zero and less than zero." But he also declared, "Should someone ask me whether I would indicate the West such as it is today as a model to my country, frankly I would have to answer negatively. . . . Through intense suffering our own country has now achieved a spiritual development of such intensity that the Western system in its present state of spiritual exhaustion does not look attractive." He maintained that "after the suffering of decades of violence and oppression, the human soul longs for things higher, warmer, and purer than those offered by today's mass living habits, introduced by the revolting invasion of publicity, by TV stupor and by intolerable music."[5]

According to Solzhenitsyn, the West has pursued physical well-being and the acquiring of material goods to the exclusion of almost everything spiritual.

"We Do Not Mind That We Die"

In 1989 we in the West were astounded by the political changes in Eastern Europe. Country after country repudiated its decades-long communist heritage and replaced its leaders with democratically elected officials. We rightly rejoiced in these changes. But we need to remember two things.

First, while the former communist lands have moved in a more democratic direction, for our part we have moved in the direction of their materialism, living as if the only thing that matters is how many earthly goods we can acquire now. We marveled at the moving scenes of East Germans passing through the openings in the infamous Berlin Wall. We saw them gazing in amazement at the abundance of goods on West Berlin shelves. But what is the good of their being able to come to the West if all they discover here is a spiritual climate vastly inferior to their own?

And that is the second thing we need to remember. Although the American media with its blindness to all things spiritual never mentioned this at the time, the changes in the Eastern Bloc did not come about by the will of any one person—Mikhail Gorbachev, Boris Yeltsin, or any other—but by the faith and spiritual vitality of the people.

For example, the strength of the Polish Solidarity movement, where the breakthrough first came, was that of the Roman Catholic Church. Pope John Paul II was a strong supporter of the people's faith and dreams.

Faith and spiritual strength also lay behind the changes in East Germany. Conventional wisdom in Germany has it that the turning point was on October 9, 1989, when seventy thousand demonstrators marched in Leipzig. The army was placed on full alert, and under normal circumstances it would have attacked the demonstrators violently. But the protestors' rallying cry was, "Let them shoot; we will still march." The army did not attack, and after that the protests grew until the government was overthrown.[6]

In Romania, where President Nicolae Ceausescu just weeks before had declared that apple trees would bear pears before socialism would be endangered in Romania, the end began in the house of a Protestant pastor whose parishioners surrounded him protectively, declaring that they were willing to die rather than let him be arrested by the state police.

Josef Tson, founder and president of the Romanian Missionary Society, who was in Romania just after the death of Ceausescu, reported the details of the story. The pastor was from the city of Timisoara, and his name was Laszlo Tokes. On Saturday, December 16, 1989, just a few days before Christmas, hundreds and then thousands of people joined the courageous parishioners who had surrounded the pastor's house and were trying to defend him. One was a twenty-four-year-old Baptist church worker whose name was Daniel Garva. He got the idea of distributing candles to the ever-growing multitude. He lit his candle, then the others lit theirs. This transformed the protective strategy into a contagious demonstration, and it was the beginning of the revolution. The next day, when the secret police opened fire on the people, Garva was shot in the leg. The doctors had to amputate his leg. But on his hospital bed this young man told his pastor, "I lost a leg, but I am happy. I lit the first light."

The people in Romania do not call the events of December 1989 a national revolution. They say, rather, "Call it God's miracle." The rallying cry of the masses was "God lives!" That from a former fiercely atheistic country! The people shouted, "Freedom! Freedom! We do not mind that we die!"[7]

Willing to die? Ah, that is the only ultimately valid test of whether one is a practical materialist at heart or whether one believes in something greater and more important than "things." Do we? No doubt there are Westerners who are willing to die for things intangible. The blacks (and others) who were willing to die for civil rights during the 1960s are examples. But today the masses of individuals in America no longer share this high standard of commitment and sacrifice.

In 1978, during President Jimmy Carter's abortive attempt to reinstate draft registration for the young, newspapers carried a photograph of a Princeton University student defiantly waving a poster marked with the words: "Nothing is worth dying for."

"But if nothing is worth dying for, is anything worth living for?" asks Charles Colson, who comments on this photograph in his book *Against the Night: Living in the New Dark Ages.*[8] If there is nothing worth living for or dying for, then the chief end of man might be cruising the malls, which is the number-one activity of today's teenagers, according to the pollsters.

Solzhenitsyn summarizes our weak thinking at this point when he says of today's Americans, "Every citizen has been granted the desired freedom and material goods in such quantity and of such quality as to guarantee in theory the achievement of happiness, in the morally inferior sense which has come into being during [these last] decades . . . So who should now renounce all this? Why and for what should one risk one's precious life in defense of common values?"[9]

Christianity has the answer to that question, and Christians in past ages have known that answer. It is to "gain a better resurrection" (Heb. 11:35), which means to do what is right because it pleases God, and pleasing God is what ultimately matters. But those who do it must be *thinking* Christians.

Thinking Beyond Ourselves

"the renewing of your mind"

There are no ordinary people. You have never talked to a mere mortal. Nations, cultures, arts, civilizations—these are mortal, and their life is to ours as the life of a gnat. But it is immortals whom we joke with, work with, marry, snub, and exploit—immortal horrors or everlasting splendors.

C. S. Lewis

The previous chapter introduced the Christian doctrines of God and revelation as the biblical answer to three of the four "isms" I had written about earlier: secularism, humanism, relativism, and materialism. The only one I did not write about explicitly was humanism, and I come to the answer to that "ism" now. The answer to humanism is the Christian doctrine of man.

Humanism is the philosophy to which human beings inevitably come if they are secularists. Secularism means eliminating from the universe God or anything else that may be transcendent, and focusing instead only on what we can see and measure now. But when God is eliminated in this process, man himself is left as the pinnacle of creation, and he becomes the inadequate and unworthy core for everything. In philosophy we usually trace the beginnings of this outlook to the pre-Socratic Greek philosopher Protagoras. Protagoras expressed his viewpoint in Greek words that have given us the better-known Latin concept *homo mensura,* which means "Man, the measure" or, as it is often expressed, "Man is the measure of all things." The idea here is that man is the norm by which everything is to be evaluated. He is the ultimate creature and thus the ultimate authority.

Although this seems to elevate man, in practice it does exactly the opposite, as we saw when we examined humanism in chapter 6. In effect, it deifies man, but this deification debases man in the end, turning him into an animal or even less than an animal. Moreover, it causes him to manipulate, ignore, disparage, wound, hate, abuse, and even murder other people.

What's Wrong with *Me*?

In the last twenty years, something terrible has happened to Americans in the way they relate to other people, and it is mainly due to the twisted humanism about which I have been writing. Prior to that time, when there was still something of a Christian ethos in this country, people used to care about and help their fellow humans. It was the normal thing to do. Today the majority of people focus on themselves and deal with others only for what they can get out of them. This approach is materialistic and utilitarian.

In 1981 a sociologist-pollster, Daniel Yankelovich, published a study of the 1970s titled *New Rules: Searching for Self-Fulfillment in a World Turned Upside Down.* This book documented a tidal shift in values by which many and eventually most Americans began to seek personal fulfillment as the ultimate goal in life, rather than operating on the principle that we are here to serve and even sacrifice for others, as Americans for the most part really had done previously.[1] He found that by the late 1970s, 72 percent of Americans spent much time thinking about themselves and their inner lives.[2] So pervasive was this change that as early as 1976, Tom Wolfe called the seventies the "Me Decade" and compared it to a third religious awakening.[3]

But what of it? Isn't this a good thing? Shouldn't thinking about ourselves make us happy? If we redirect our energy to fulfilling ourselves and earn as much as we can to indulge even our tiniest desires, shouldn't we be satisfied with life? No! It doesn't work that way, as we have discovered. It fails on the personal level, and it also fails in the area of our relationships with other people.

In 1978 Margaret Halsey wrote an article for *Newsweek* magazine titled "What's Wrong With Me, Me, Me?" It was a good article, and even the title was illuminating. Halsey referred to Wolfe's description of the people of the seventies as a "me" generation, who believed that "inside every human being, however unprepossessing, there is a glorious, talented and overwhelmingly attractive personality [which] will be revealed in all its splendor if the individual just forgets about courtesy, cooperativeness and consideration for others and proceeds to do exactly what he or she feels like doing."[4]

The problem, as Halsey pointed out, is not that there are not attractive characteristics in everyone (or at least in most people), but that human nature consists even more basically of "a mess of unruly primitive elements" that spoil the "self-discovery." These unruly elements need to be overcome, not indulged. And this means that the attractive personalities we seek to discover really are not there to be discovered but, rather, are natures that need to be *developed* through choices, hard work, and lasting commitments to others. When we ask "What's wrong with me?" it is the "me, me, me" that is the problem.

The emphasis on self-discovery affects our relations with other people, too, because, in spite of what humanism seems to promise, it makes our world impersonal. Charles Reich wrote in his best-selling book *The Greening of America,* "Modern living has obliterated place, locality and neighborhood, and given us the anonymous separateness of our existence. The family, the most basic social system, has been ruthlessly stripped to its functional essentials. Friendship has been coated over with a layer of impenetrable artificiality as men strive to live roles designed for them. Protocol, competition, hostility and fear have replaced the warmth of the circle of affection which might sustain man against a hostile environment." He said that "America [has become] one vast, terrifying anti-community."[5]

The Christian Doctrine of Man

The Christian answer to this is the biblical doctrine of man, which means that if we are to have renewed minds in this area, we need to stop thinking about ourselves and other people in the same way the world thinks of itself and others and instead begin operating within a biblical framework.

But what does that mean? Well, when we turn to the Bible to see what it has to say about human beings, we find two surprising things. First, we find that, according to the Bible, man is far more important and more valuable than the humanists imagine him to be. Man is a uniquely valuable being. But, second, in his fallen condition we also find that he is much worse than the humanists suppose.

Let's first examine the fact that human beings are more valuable than humanists imagine. The Bible teaches this at the very beginning of Genesis when it reports God as saying, "Let us make man in our image, in our likeness" (Gen. 1:26). We are then told, "So God created man in his own image, in the image of God he created him; male and female he created them" (v. 27).

Books in ancient times were copied by hand with rough lettering. There was no typesetting, and it was not feasible to emphasize one idea over another by such devices as italics, capital letters, boldface, and centered headings. Instead, emphasis was made by repetition. For example, when Jesus wanted to stress something as unusually important, he began with the words "verily, verily" or "truly, truly," a repetition. We have exactly the same thing in the first chapter of Genesis with the words "in our image," "in his own image," and "in the image of God." That idea is repeated three times, which is a way of saying that our being created in God's image is important. It is what makes us distinct from the animals, and we should value this highly.

Just a few chapters further on in Genesis, the fact that human beings are made in God's image is the reason given for why we are not to murder other people and why murderers should themselves be punished by death, since they devalued another individual's life, taking it lightly: "Whoever sheds the blood of man, by man shall his blood be shed; for in the image of God has God made man" (Gen. 9:6).

What does it mean to be made in the image of God? Bible students have debated the full meaning of that for centuries, which is not surprising, since being made in God's image means to be like God, and God is above and beyond us, far beyond our full understanding. Yet the situation is not hopeless. Here are some things we can point to.

1. *Personality*. To be made in God's image means to possess the attributes of personality, as God himself does, but animals, plants, and inorganic matter do not. This involves knowledge, memory, feelings, and a will. Of course, there is a sense in which animals possess what we call personalities, meaning that individuals in a species sometimes have behavior patterns that differ from others in the same species. But animals do not create. They do not love or worship. Personality, in the sense I am writing about here, is something that links human beings to God but does not link either God or man to the rest of creation.

2. *Morality*. The second facet of being made in the image of God is morality, for God is a moral God, and anyone made in his image is made with the capacity of discerning between what is right and wrong, between good and evil. This involves the further elements of freedom and responsibility. To be sure, the freedom of human beings is not absolute, as God's freedom is. We are not free to do all things. We are limited. Nevertheless, our freedom is a true freedom, even when we use it wrongly. Adam and Eve used their freedom wrongly when they sinned. They lost their original righteousness as a result. But they were still free to sin, and they were free in their sinful state afterward in the sense that they were still able to make right and wrong choices. Moreover, they continued to be responsible for those choices.

3. *Spirituality*. The third part of being made in the image of God is spirituality, which means that human

beings are able to have fellowship with God. Another way of saying this is to say that "God is spirit" (John 4:24) and that we are also spirits meant for eternal fellowship with him. Nothing can be greater than that for human beings, and the Westminster Shorter Catechism says it well when it replies in the answer to the first question that "man's chief end is to glorify God and to enjoy him forever."

Perhaps at this point you are beginning to see why secular humanism is so bad and not just a "less attractive" option than Christianity. Although humanism sounds like it is focusing on man and elevating man, it actually strips away the most valuable parts of human nature. As far as personality goes, it reduces us to mere animal urges, as Sigmund Freud tried to do. As far as morality goes, instead of remaining responsible moral agents, which is our glory, we are turned into mere products of our environment and/or our genetic makeup, as behavioral psychologist B. F. Skinner asserts. As far as spirituality is concerned, well, how can we maintain a relationship to God if there is no God and we are made the measure of all things?

To refer again to Aleksandr Solzhenitsyn, in humanism "things higher, warmer, and purer" are drowned out by "today's mass living habits and TV stupor." We can make engrossing TV videos or commercials, but we no longer build cathedrals.

The Doctrine of the Fall

What is the problem, then? If human beings are more important and more valuable than the humanists imagine, why is it that conditions in the world are so bad? The answer is the Christian doctrine of sin, which tells us that although people are more valuable than secularists imagine, they are in worse trouble than the humanists can admit. We have been made in God's image, but we have lost that image, which means that we are no longer fully human or as human as God intends us to be. We are fallen creatures.

Here I think of Psalm 8, the psalm that both begins and ends with the words: "O LORD, our Lord, how majestic is your name in all the earth!" (vv. 1, 9). In the middle it talks about the created order. So the beginning and ending teach that everything begins and ends with God, rather than with man, and that if we think clearly we will agree with this.

Then, in verses 3 through 7, it describes men and women particularly.

> When I consider your heavens,
>   the work of your fingers,
> the moon and the stars,
>   which you have set in place,
> what is man that you are mindful of him,
>   the son of man that you care for him?
> You made him a little lower than the heavenly beings
>   and crowned him with glory and honor.
> You made him ruler over the works of your hands;
>   you put everything under his feet:
> all flocks and herds,
>   and the beasts of the field.

These verses fix man at a very interesting place in the created order: lower than the angels ("the heavenly beings") but higher than the animals—somewhere between. This is what Thomas Aquinas saw when he described man as a mediating being. He is like the angels in that he has a soul. But he is like the beasts in that he has a body. The angels have souls but not bodies, while the animals have bodies but not souls.

But here is the point. Although man is a mediating being, created to be somewhere between the angels and the animals, in Psalm 8 he is nevertheless described as being somewhat lower than the angels rather than as being somewhat higher than the beasts, which means that he is destined to look not downward to the beasts, but upward to the angels and beyond them to God and so to become increasingly like him. However, if we will not look up, if we reject God, as secularism does, then we will inevitably look downward and so become increasingly like the lower creatures and behave like them. We will become beastlike, which is exactly what is happening in our society. People are acting like animals, or even worse.

Over the last few decades I have noticed that our culture is tending to justify bad human behavior on the ground that we are, after all, "just animals." I saw an article in a scientific journal about a certain kind of duck. Two scientists had been observing a family of these ducks, and they reported something in this duck family that they called "gang rape." I am sure the scientists did not want to excuse this crime among humans by the comparison they were making, but they were suggesting that gang rape among humans is at least understandable, given our animal ancestry. The inference comes from the evolutionary, naturalistic world view they espoused.

A story of a similar nature appeared in the September 6, 1982, issue of *Newsweek* magazine. It was accompanied by a picture of an adult baboon holding a dead infant baboon, and over this was a headline that read: "Biologists Say Infanticide Is as Normal as the Sex Drive—And That Most Animals, Including Man, Practice It." The title is as revealing in its way as Carl Sagan's "The cosmos is all that is or ever was or ever will be." It identifies man as an animal, and it justifies his behavior on the basis of that identification. The sequence of thought goes like this: (1) Man is an animal; (2) Animals kill their offspring; (3) Therefore, it is all right (or at least understandable) that human beings kill their offspring.

The argument is fallacious, of course. Most animals do not kill their offspring. They protect their young and care for them. But even if in a few instances some animals do kill their offspring, this is still not comparable to the crimes of which human beings are capable. In this country alone we kill over one and a half million babies each year by abortion—usually just for the convenience of the mother. And the incidence of abuse and outright murders of children is soaring.

Still another story appeared in the June 1992 issue of *Discover* magazine. It was titled "What's Love Got to Do with It?" and it was a description of variant sex practices, including homosexuality, among bonobos, a rare species of chimplike apes. A subhead read, "Sex is fun. Sex makes them feel good and keeps the group together." The obvious message is that if a variety of sexual experiences is good for the apes—and "sex makes them feel good and keeps the group together"—it should be good for humans, too. "Make love, not war!" is the article's moral.

Never mind that sex crimes are soaring among us, keeping pace with our so-called sexual liberation. Or that bonobos are hardly typical even of the animal world.

The Doctrine of Redemption

Renewing our minds begins with understanding and applying the great Christian doctrines, and thus far we have at least touched on four of them: the doctrines of God, revelation, man, and the fall. These doctrines are not exhaustive, but they are very important as well as being a proper starting place for our thinking if we are serious about what Paul is urging upon us in our text from Romans: "Be transformed by the renewing of your mind."

But there is one other doctrine we need to mention without which nothing in the previous studies would be complete: the doctrine of redemption.

Redemption means that "God so loved the world that he gave his one and only Son, that whoever believes in him shall not perish but have eternal life" (John 3:16), and it infinitely intensifies everything I have been saying about man being both more valuable than the humanists can imagine as well as also being worse than they can possibly suppose.

The doctrine of redemption intensifies man's value, because it teaches that even in his fallen state, a condition in which he hates God and kills his fellow creatures, man is still so valuable to God that God planned for and carried out the death of his own precious Son to save him.

At the same time, the doctrine of redemption teaches that man's state is indescribably dreadful, because it took nothing less than the death of the very Son of God to accomplish it.

I want to close by referring to what I regard as the greatest single piece of writing produced by the great Christian scholar and apologist C. S. Lewis. It was preached as a sermon in the summer of 1941, but is known to us as an essay called "The Weight of Glory."[6] Lewis began by probing for the meaning of glory, recognizing that it is something of the very essence of God that we desire. It is something "no natural happiness will satisfy." At the same time it is also something from which we, in our sinful state, have been shut out. We want it. We sense that we are destined for it. But glory is beyond us—apart from what God has done to save us and make us like himself.

At the end of the essay, Lewis applied this to how we should learn to think about other people. We should understand that they are either going to be brought into glory, which is a supreme and indescribable blessing, or else they are going to be shut out from it—forever. Here he says:

It is a serious thing to live in a society of possible gods and goddesses, to remember that the dullest and most uninteresting person you can talk to may one day be a creature which, if you saw it now, you would be strongly tempted to worship, or else a horror and a corruption such as you now meet, if at all, only in a nightmare. . . . There are no *ordinary* people. You have never talked to a mere mortal. Nations, cultures, arts, civilizations— these are mortal, and their life is to ours as the life of a gnat. But it is immortals whom we joke with, work with, marry, snub, and exploit—immortal horrors or everlasting splendors.[7]

What Lewis was doing in that essay was helping us to develop a Christian mind about other people, what I have been discussing in this chapter. And his bottom line was that we will treat others better if we learn to think of them in the Bible's terms.

Check It Out

"God's . . . *good, pleasing and perfect* will"

Of the fashion of the world, it may truly be said that the more you try it, the less you will find it to be satisfying. . . . It is altogether otherwise with the will of God. That often looks worst at the beginning. It seems hard and dark. But on! On with you in the proving of it! Prove it patiently, perseveringly, with prayer and pains. And you will get growing clearness, light, enlargement, joy.

Robert S. Candlish

Some time ago, the staff of "The Bible Study Hour" prepared a brochure that compared the world's thinking and the Bible's teaching in six important areas:

God, man, the Bible, money, sex, and success. The differences were striking, but what impressed me most as I read the brochure is how right many of the world's ideas seem if we are not thinking critically and in a biblical way. This is because we hear the world's approach so often, so attractively, and so persuasively, especially on television.

Here are some of "the world's" statements we printed:

"I matter most, and the world exists to serve me. Whatever satisfies me is what's important."

"If I earn enough money, I'll be happy. I need money to provide security for myself and my family. Financial security will protect me from hardship."

"Anything is acceptable as long as it doesn't hurt another person."

"Success is the path to fame, wealth, pleasure and power. Look out for number one."

How about the Christian way? From the world's perspective, the Christian way does not look attractive or even right. It says such things as: "God is in control of all things and has a purpose for everything that happens. . . . Man exists to glorify God. . . . Money cannot shield us against heartbreak, failure, sin, disease, or disaster. . . . Success in God's kingdom means humility and service to others." Because we are so much part of the world and so little like Jesus Christ, even Christians find God's way unappealing. Nevertheless, we are to press on in that way and prove by our lives that the will of God really is "good, pleasing and perfect" in all things.

I find it significant that this is where Paul's statements about being transformed by the renewing of our minds, rather than being conformed to the patterns of this world, end. They end with proving the way of God to be the best way and the will of God to be perfect.

This means that action is needed. Or, to say it differently, God is not producing hothouse or ivory-tower

Christians. God is forming people who will prove the value of his way by conscious choices and deliberate obedience.

One of the best exegetes of the last century was a Scottish pastor named Robert Candlish. He wrote a book on Romans 12, in which he made this point well. Candlish said:

> The believer's transformation by the renewing of his mind is not the ultimate end which the Holy Spirit seeks in his regenerating and renovating work. It is the immediate and primary design of that work, in one sense. We are created anew in Christ Jesus. That new creation is what the Holy Spirit first aims at and effects. But "we are created in Christ Jesus unto good works, which God hath before ordained that we should walk in them" (Eph. 2:10). The essence of a good work is the doing of the will of God. The proving of the will of God, therefore, is a fitting sequel of our "being transformed by the renewing of our mind."[1]

God Has a Will for Each of Us

This last part of Romans 12:1–2 is not difficult to handle, because the points are obvious. The first is this: God has a good, pleasing, and perfect will for each of us. Otherwise, how would it be possible for us to test and approve what that will is?

But this requires some explanation. Today, when Christians talk about discovering the will of God, what they usually have in mind is praying until God somehow discloses a specific direction for their lives—whom they should marry, what job they should take, whether or not they should be missionaries, what house they should buy, and such things. This is not exactly what proving the will of God means, nor is it what Romans

12:2 is teaching. The will of God is far more important than that.

Garry Friesen, a professor at Multnomah School of the Bible, and J. Robin Maxson, a pastor from Klamath, Oregon, wrote a very good book on the subject of knowing God's will, entitled *Decision Making & the Will of God.*[2] In that book they distinguish among three meanings of the word *will:* first, God's *sovereign will,* which is hidden and is not revealed to us except as it unfolds in history; second, God's *moral will,* which is revealed in Scripture; and third, God's *specific will for individuals,* which is what people are usually thinking about when they speak of searching for or finding God's will. These authors rightly accept the first two of these "wills." But they disagree with the idea that God has a specific will for each life and that it is the duty of the individual believer to find that will or "live in the center of it."

My evaluation of this book is that it is helpful in cutting away many of the hang-ups that have nearly incapacitated some Christians. Its exposure of the weakness of subjective methods of determining guidance is astute. Its stress on the sufficiency of Scripture in all moral matters is essential. My only reservation is that it does not seem to me to acknowledge that God does indeed have a specific (though usually hidden) will for us or adequately recognize that God does sometimes reveal that will in special situations.

We may not know what that specific will is.

We do not need to be under pressure to "discover" it, fearing that if we miss it, somehow we will be doomed to a life outside the center of God's will or to his "second best."

We are free to make decisions with what light and wisdom we possess.

Nevertheless, we can know that God does have a perfect will for us, that the Holy Spirit is praying for us in accordance with that will, and that this will of God for us will be done—because God has decreed it and because the Holy Spirit is praying for us in this area.

Still, having said all this, I need to add that this is not primarily what Romans 12:2 is talking about when it speaks of God's will. In this verse "will" is to be interpreted in its context, and the context indicates that the will of God that we are encouraged to follow is the general will of offering our bodies to God as living sacrifices, refusing to be conformed to the world's ways, and instead being transformed from within by the renewing of our minds. It is this that we are to pursue and thus find to be good, pleasing, and perfect, though, of course, if we do it, we will also find ourselves working out the details of God's specific will for our lives.

Good, Pleasing, and Perfect

The second obvious point about the ending of Romans 12:2 is that the will of God that we are talking about is "good, pleasing and perfect." In other words, it teaches about the nature of God's will for us as well as the fact that God has one.

1. *The will of God is good.* In a general way, the will of God for every Christian, regardless of who he or she is, is revealed in the Bible. Romans 8 contains a broad expression of this plan: that we might be delivered from God's judgment upon us for our sin and instead be made increasingly like Jesus Christ. The five specifically highlighted steps of this plan include: (1) foreknowledge, (2) predestination, (3) effectual calling, (4) justification, and (5) glorification (vv. 29–30).

But there are also many specifics.

The Ten Commandments contain some of these. It is God's will that we have no other gods before him, that we do not worship even him by the use of images, that

we do not misuse his name, that we remember the Sab-
bath day by keeping it holy, that we honor our parents,
that we do not murder or commit adultery or steal or
give false testimony or covet (Exod. 20:3–17). The Lord
Jesus Christ amplified upon many of these commandments and added others, above all teaching that we are
to "love each other" (John 15:12).

It is God's will that we be holy (1 Thess. 4:3).

It is God's will that we should pray (1 Thess. 5:17).

These directives often do not appeal to us, because
our minds and hearts are often far from God and we are
thinking in the world's way. Nevertheless, they are
"good" instructions, which we will discover if we will
obey God in these areas and put his will into practice.
As one of the great Romans commentators, Robert Haldane, says, "The will of God is here distinguished as
good, because, however much the mind may be opposed
to it and how much soever we may think that it curtails
our pleasures and mars our enjoyments, obedience to
God conduces to our happiness."[3]

2. *The will of God is pleasing.* Pleasing to whom? Not
to God, of course. That is obvious. Besides, we do not
have to prove that God is pleased by his own will, nor
could we. When Paul encourages us to prove that God's
will is a pleasing will, he obviously means pleasing to
us. That is, if we determine to walk in God's way, refusing to be conformed to the world and being transformed
instead by the renewing of our minds, we will not have
to fear that at the end of our lives we will look back and
be dissatisfied or bitter, judging our lives to have been
an utter waste. On the contrary, we will look back and
conclude that our lives were worthwhile and be satisfied with them.

I was once talking with a Christian man whose mother
was dying. The mother was not a Christian, and she had
become very bitter, although she had not been a bitter

person before her illness. She felt that everyone was turning against her, even her children, who actually were only trying to help her. This man said to me, "I am convinced that Christians and non-Christians come to the end of their lives very differently. Those who are not Christians feel that they do not deserve to end their lives with failing health and pain, and they think their lives have been wasted. Christians are satisfied with what God has led them through and has done for them. It is better to die as a Christian."

I think that is exactly right. It is what Paul is saying.

3. *The will of God is perfect.* A number of words in the Greek language are translated by the English word "perfect." One is *akribôs,* from which we get our word "accurate," meaning "correct." Another is *katartizô,* which means "well fitted" to a specific end, like the completion of a puzzle. The word in Romans 12:2 is different. It is *teleios,* which has the thought of something that has attained its full end or is "complete." It can be used of one who is mature, a mature adult. It is used of Jesus, who became a complete or perfect man. It is used of the end of history. In our text it means that those who do the will of God discover that it is not lacking in any respect. There is a satisfying wholeness about God's will.

To put this in negative form, it means that if we reach the end of our lives and are dissatisfied with them, this will only mean that we have been living in the world's way and have been conformed to it, rather than having been transformed by the renewing of our minds. We will have been living for ourselves rather than for God and others.

We Need to Check It Out

The third obvious point of this verse is that we need to prove by our experience that the will of God is indeed what Paul tells us it is: "good, pleasing and perfect." To use our normal way of speaking, we need to check it out. Moreover, it is by checking it out that we will begin to find out what it actually is.

This is the exact opposite of our normal way of thinking. Usually we want God to tell us what his will for us is, and after that we want to be able to decide whether it is "good, pleasing and perfect," and thus whether or not we want to do it. Romans 12:2 tells us that we have to start living in God's way and that it is only as we do that we will begin to know God's will in its fullness and learn how good it really is. Robert Candlish says rightly, "The will of God . . . can be known only by trial. . . . No one who is partaker of a finite nature and who occupies the position of a subject or servant under the authority of God, under his law, can understand what . . . the will of God is otherwise than through actual experience. You cannot explain to him beforehand what the will of God is and what are its attributes or characteristics. He must learn this for himself. And he must learn it experimentally. He must prove in his own person and in his own personal history what is . . . 'that good and acceptable and perfect will of God.'"[4]

God's Creatures and Probation

Speaking of Candlish, let me say that in my opinion one of the most valuable parts of his study is the way he follows up on this idea, noting that the idea of proving the will of God "experimentally" goes a long way toward explaining the Bible's teaching about probation. This word is derived from the word *prove* and refers to a trial or test. According to Candlish, every order of free and intelligent being has been called upon to stand trial in the sense that ultimately it was created to prove that the will of God is good, pleasing, and perfect. Or, if the

creature should reject that will and fail the test, to prove
that the contrary will of the world is disappointing and
defective. Candlish reminds us of the following biblical examples.

1. *The angels.* We are not told much about the trial of
the angels in the Bible, but it is certain that they did stand
trial and that some of them, even a large part of that
nearly innumerable host, failed that trial and so entered
into the rebellion led by Satan and passed under the
severe judgment of Almighty God.

Candlish speculates that the specific issue of that trial
may have been the command to worship the Son of God:
"When God brings his firstborn into the world, he says,
'Let all God's angels worship him'" (Heb. 1:6). Whether
or not this was the specific matter the angels of God were
to prove good, pleasing, and perfect, it is clear that many
did not regard God's will as such. They rebelled against
it, and even those who did adhere to God's will must
have adhered to it not knowing then the full goodness,
satisfaction, or perfection of what they were being called
upon to do. They have been learning it since by their
doing of it, that is, they have been learning it experimentally (cf. Eph. 3:8–11).

2. *Man in his pristine state.* The second case of probation is man in his pristine state. We know a great deal
more about this than we do about the trial of the angels,
since it concerns us most directly and is revealed to us
for that reason. Adam and Eve were required to prove
the good, pleasing, and perfect will of God in the matter
of the tree of the knowledge of good and evil, refusing
to eat of it because God had forbidden it to them. We
know how this turned out. When weighed against what
they considered to be more desirable ("you will be like
God, knowing good and evil," Gen. 3:5), they chose the
way of sin, ate of the tree, and through death paid the
price of their transgression.

Candlish argues that if our first parents had kept the will of God, though it did not seem desirable at that stage of their lives, "they would have found by experience that what God announced to them as his will was really in itself, as the seal of his previous covenant of life and as the preparation for the unfolding of his higher providence, fair, reasonable [and] good. . . . They would have learned experimentally that it was suited to their case and circumstances, deserving of their acceptance, sure to become more and more pleasing as they entered more and more into its spirit and became more and more thoroughly reconciled to the quiet simplicity of submission which it fostered."[5]

All this and more! But they did not prove it to be such and therefore brought sin, judgment, and death on the human race. We continue to suffer from their erroneous and foolish choice today.

3. *The Lord Jesus Christ.* The third example of probation is Jesus Christ, not a creature to be sure, but nevertheless one who in his incarnate state took it upon himself to prove that God's will was indeed good, pleasing, and perfect, even though it involved the pain of the cross, which in itself hardly seemed good, pleasing, or acceptable.

Jesus prayed in the garden that the cross might be taken from him, adding, "Yet not as I will, but as you will" (Matt. 26:39). The author of Hebrews says, "During the days of Jesus' life on earth, he offered up prayers and petitions with loud cries and tears to the one who could save him from death, and he was heard because of his reverent submission. Although he was a son, he learned obedience from what he suffered" (Heb. 5:7–8). In his letter to the Philippians, Paul speaks of Jesus' humbling himself and becoming "obedient to death—even death on a cross!" (Phil. 2:8).

Writes Candlish, "It must have been, it often was, with him a struggle—an effort—to do the will of God. It was not easy, it was not pleasant. It was self-denial, self-sacrifice, self-crucifixion throughout. It was repulsive to the highest and holiest instincts of his pure humanity. It laid upon him most oppressive burdens; it brought him into most distressing scenes; it involved him in ceaseless, often thankless toil; it exposed him to all sorts of uncongenial encounters with evil men and evil angels. But he proved it. And in the proving of it, and as he was proving it, he found it to be good and acceptable and perfect."[6]

4. *Christians.* And what of ourselves, we who confess Jesus Christ to be our Lord and Savior? We are on trial now, and the matter of our probation is whether or not we will embrace the will of God for our lives, turning from the world and its ways, and so prove by the very embracing of that will that it is exactly what God declares it to be when he calls it perfect.

Who is to do that? *You* are, and you are to do it in the precise earthly circumstances into which God has placed you.

How are you to do it? You are to do it *experimentally,* that is, by actually putting the revealed will of God to the test.

When are you to do it? *Right now and tomorrow and the day after that.* That is, you are to do it repeatedly and consistently and faithfully all through your life until the day of your death or until Jesus comes again.

Why are you to do it? Because it is *the right thing to do,* and because the will of God really is good, pleasing, and perfect.

Candlish says:

Of the fashion of the world, it may truly be said that the more you try it, the less you will find it to be satisfying.

It looks well; it looks fair, at first. But who that has lived long has not found it to be vanity at last?

It is altogether otherwise with the will of God. That often looks worst at the beginning. It seems hard and dark. But on! On with you in the proving of it! Prove it patiently, perseveringly, with prayer and pains. And you will get growing clearness, light, enlargement, joy. You will more and more find that "the path of the just is as the shining light, that shineth more and more unto the perfect day." For "wisdom's ways are ways of pleasantness, and all her paths are peace." "The judgments of the Lord are true and righteous altogether. More to be desired are they than gold, yea, than much fine gold; sweeter also than honey, and the honeycomb. Moreover by them is thy servant warned; and in keeping of them there is great reward."[7]

"Therefore, I urge you, brothers, in view of God's mercy, to offer your bodies as living sacrifices, holy and pleasing to God—this is your spiritual act of worship. Do not conform any longer to the pattern of this world, but be transformed by the renewing of your mind. Then you will be able to test and approve what God's will is— his good, pleasing and perfect will" (Rom. 12:1–2).

Notes

Chapter 1

1. Harry Blamires, *The Christian Mind: How Should a Christian Think?* (Ann Arbor, Mich.: Servant Books, 1978). Original edition 1963.

2. John Murray, *The Epistle to the Romans*, 2 vols. in 1 (Grand Rapids: Wm. B. Eerdmans, 1968), vol. 2, p. 109.

3. Francis A. Schaeffer, *How Should We Then Live? The Rise and Decline of Western Thought and Culture* (Old Tappan, N.J.: Fleming H. Revell, 1976), p. 252.

4. Ibid., p. 256.

5. Carl F. H. Henry, *Twilight of a Great Civilization* (Westchester, Ill.: Crossway Books, 1988), p. 170.

6. Allan Bloom, *The Closing of the American Mind* (New York: Simon and Schuster, 1987).

7. John Calvin, *The Epistles of Paul the Apostle to the Romans and to the Thessalonians*, trans. Ross MacKenzie (Grand Rapids: Wm. B. Eerdmans, 1973), p. 262.

8. Charles Hodge, *A Commentary on Romans* (Edinburgh and Carlisle, Pa.: The Banner of Truth Trust, 1972), p. 393. Original edition 1835.

9. Leon Morris, *The Epistle to the Romans* (Grand Rapids: Wm. B. Eerdmans, and Leicester, England: Inter-Varsity Press, 1988), p. 431.

10. George Gallup, Jr., "Is America's Faith for Real?" in Princeton Theological Seminary *Alumni News* 22, no. 4 (Summer 1982): 15–17.

Chapter 2

1. See Romans 6:1–14; Galatians 2:20; 5:24; Philippians 3:10; Colossians 3:3–5; 2 Timothy 2:11.

2. John Calvin, *The Epistles of Paul the Apostle to the Romans and to the Thessalonians*, trans. Ross MacKenzie (Grand Rapids: Wm. B. Eerdmans, 1973), p. 262.

3. See James Montgomery Boice, *Romans*, vol. 2, *The Reign of Grace: Romans 5:1–8:39* (Grand Rapids: Baker Book House, 1992), pp. 651–653, 677.

Chapter 3

1. Robert S. Candlish, *Studies in Romans 12: The Christian's Sacrifice and Service of Praise* (Grand Rapids: Kregel Publications, 1989), pp. 33, 34.

2. John Calvin, *The Epistles of Paul the Apostle to the Romans and to the Thessalonians*, trans. Ross MacKenzie (Grand Rapids: Wm. B. Eerdmans, 1973), p. 264.

3. Leon Morris, *The Epistle to the Romans* (Grand Rapids: Wm. B. Eerdmans, and Leicester, England: Inter-Varsity Press, 1988), pp. 433, 434.

4. Robert Haldane, *An Exposition of the Epistle to the Romans* (MacDill AFB: MacDonald Publishing, 1958), p. 554. See also John Murray, *The Epistle to the Romans*, 2 vols. in 1 (Grand Rapids: Wm. B. Eerdmans, 1968), vol. 2, p. 111. Murray notes the depreciation of the body in favor of the spirit in Greek thought and argues that against that background an emphasis upon the body by Paul was a Christian necessity.

5. See Mike Bellah, *Baby Boom Believers: Why We Think We Need It All and How to Survive When We Don't Get It* (Wheaton, Ill.: Tyndale House, 1988), p. 27.

6. Handley C. G. Moule, *The Epistle of St. Paul to the Romans* (London: Hodder and Stoughton, 1896), pp. 324, 325.

7. J. I. Packer, *Rediscovering Holiness* (Ann Arbor, Mich.: Servant Publications, 1992), pp. 12, 13.

8. J. C. Ryle, *Holiness: Its Nature, Hindrances, Difficulties and Roots* (Cambridge: James Clark, 1959), and Jerry Bridges, *The Pursuit of Holiness* (Colorado Springs: NavPress, 1978). Lately a number of important books have approached holiness from the side of the spiritual disciplines: R. Kent Hughes, *Disciplines of a Godly Man* (Wheaton, Ill.: Crossway Books, 1991); Dallas Willard, *The Spirit of the Disciplines: Understanding How God Changes Lives* (San Francisco: Harper & Row, 1988); and Donald S. Whitney, *Spiritual Disciplines for the Christian Life* (Colorado Springs: NavPress, 1991).

Chapter 4

1. Dale Carnegie, *How to Win Friends and Influence People* (New York: Simon and Schuster, 1963), pp. 173–176.

2. J. I. Packer, *Rediscovering Holiness* (Ann Arbor, Mich.: Servant Publications, 1992), p. 75.

3. John Calvin, *The Epistles of Paul the Apostle to the Romans and to the Thessalonians*, trans. Ross MacKenzie (Grand Rapids: Wm. B. Eerdmans, 1973), p. 263.

4. Arthur W. Pink, *The Attributes of God* (Grand Rapids: Baker Book House, n.d.), pp. 83, 84.

Chapter 5

1. John Murray, *The Epistle to the Romans*, 2 vols. in 1 (Grand Rapids: Wm. B. Eerdmans, 1968), vol. 2, p. 112.

2. Ibid. Leon Morris says, "Today most interpreters understand the adjective as *spiritual*, which makes good sense and is certainly in mind. But it is hard to think that the connection with 'reason' has been completely lost, and there is something to be said for 'intelligent worship' (Phillips) or JB's 'that is worthy of thinking beings'" (Leon Morris, *The Epistle to the Romans* [Grand Rapids: Wm. B. Eerdmans, and Leicester, England: Inter-Varsity Press, 1988], p. 434). The New American Standard Bible translates the words as "spiritual service," but the New English Bible by a longer phrasing probably comes closest to the meaning by saying "worship offered by the mind and the heart."

Chapter 6

1. R. C. Sproul, *Lifeviews: Understanding the Ideas that Shape Society Today* (Old Tappan, N. J.: Fleming H. Revell, 1986), p. 35.

2. Harry Blamires, *The Christian Mind: How Should a Christian Think?* (Ann Arbor, Mich.: Servant Books, 1963), p. 44.

3. *Humanist Manifestos I and II* (New York: Prometheus Books, 1973), p. 13.

4. Ibid., p. 16.

5. Ibid., p. 17.

6. Herbert Schlossberg, *Idols for Destruction: Christian Faith and Its Confrontation with American Society* (Washington, D.C.: Regnery Gateway, 1990).

7. Allan Bloom, *The Closing of the American Mind* (New York: Simon and Schuster, 1987), p. 25.

8. *Time,* May 25, 1987, p. 14.

Chapter 7

1. Ted Koppel, "Viewpoints," Commencement Address, Duke University, May 10, 1987.

2. Neil Postman, *Amusing Ourselves to Death: Public Discourse in the Age of Show Business* (New York: Penguin Books, 1986). First edition 1985.

3. Ibid., pp. vii, viii.

4. Ibid., p. 100.

5. Ibid., p. 125.

6. From memorandums prepared by William Gavin. Quoted by Joe McGinniss, *The Selling of the President* (New York: Penguin Books, 1988), pp. 208, 188, 189. Original edition 1969.

7. Postman, *Amusing Ourselves to Death,* pp. 116, 117.

8. Ibid., p. 123.

9. John R. W. Stott, *Your Mind Matters: The Place of the Mind in the Christian Life* (Downers Grove, Ill: InterVarsity Press, 1972), p. 26.

Chapter 8

1. Harry Blamires, *The Christian Mind: How Should a Christian Think?* (Ann Arbor, Mich.: Servant Books, 1978), p. 45. Original edition 1963.

2. John H. Gerstner, "Man as God Made Him" in James M. Boice, ed., *Our Savior God: Man, Christ and the Atonement* (Grand Rapids: Baker Book House, 1980), p. 20.

3. Francis A. Schaeffer, *He Is There and He Is Not Silent* (Wheaton, Ill.: Tyndale House, 1972).

4. Blamires, *The Christian Mind,* p. 141.

5. Aleksandr Solzhenitsyn, "A World Split Apart," The 1978 Commencement Address at Harvard University, *Harvard Gazette,* June 8, 1978, pp. 17–19.

6. The generally neglected story of the role of the church in the changes that have come to Eastern Europe is told in part in the January 22, 1990, issue of *National Review,* "How the East Was Won: Reports on the Rebirth of Christianity under Communism," pp. 22-28.

7. *Voice of Truth* magazine, Romanian Missionary Society, January-February 1990 issue, p. 2.

8. Charles Colson, *Against the Night: Living in the New Dark Ages* (Ann Arbor, Mich.: Servant Publications, 1989), p. 33.

9. Solzhenitsyn, "A World Split Apart," p. 17.

Chapter 9

1. Daniel Yankelovich, *New Rules: Searching for Self-Fulfillment in a World Turned Upside Down* (New York: Random House, 1981), pp. 10, 11.

2. Ibid., p. 5.

3. Tom Wolfe, "The 'Me Decade' and the Third Great Awakening," *New York* magazine, August 23, 1976, pp. 26–40.

4. *Newsweek,* April 17, 1978, p. 25.

5. Charles Reich, *The Greening of America: The Coming of a New Consciousness and the Rebirth of a Future* (New York: Bantam Books, 1971), p. 7.

6. C. S. Lewis, "The Weight of Glory" in *The Weight of Glory and Other Addresses* (New York: Macmillan/Collier Books, 1980).

7. Ibid., pp. 18, 19.

Chapter 10

1. Robert S. Candlish, *Studies in Romans 12: The Christian's Sacrifice and Service of Praise* (Grand Rapids: Kregel Publications, 1989), pp. 80, 81. Original edition 1867.

2. Garry Friesen with J. Robin Maxson, *Decision Making & the Will of God: An Alternative to the Traditional View* (Portland: Multnomah Press, 1980).

3. Robert Haldane, *An Exposition of the Epistle to the Romans* (MacDill AFB: MacDonald Publishing, 1958), p. 557.

4. Candlish, *Studies in Romans 12,* p. 81.

5. Ibid., p. 85.

6. Ibid., p. 89.

7. Ibid., pp. 96, 97.